THE THINGS THEY CANNOT SAY

ALSO BY KEVIN SITES

In the Hot Zone

THE THINGS THEY CANNOT SAY

STORIES SOLDIERS WON'T TELL YOU ABOUT WHAT THEY'VE SEEN, DONE OR FAILED TO DO IN WAR

KEVIN SITES

COUNTY LIBRARY
DISCARD
TILLAMOOK, ORE.

HARPER  PERENNIAL

NEW YORK • LONDON • TORONTO • SYDNEY • NEW DELHI • AUCKLAND

HARPER PERENNIAL

THE THINGS THEY CANNOT SAY. Copyright © 2013 by Kevin Sites. All rights reserved.
Printed in the United States of America. No part of this book may be used or
reproduced in any manner whatsoever without written permission except in the case
of brief quotations embodied in critical articles and reviews. For information address
HarperCollins Publishers, 10 East 53rd Street, New York, NY 10022.

HarperCollins books may be purchased for educational, business, or sales promotional
use. For information please write: Special Markets Department, HarperCollins
Publishers, 10 East 53rd Street, New York, NY 10022.

FIRST EDITION

Designed by Lisa Stokes

Library of Congress Cataloging-in-Publication Data is available upon request.

ISBN 978-0-06-199052-6

13 14 15 16 17   OV/RRD   10 9 8 7 6 5 4 3 2 1

This book is dedicated to my wife, Anita, and the rest of the "party of five," Tina, Cami and Vae, for giving me the gift of being necessary.

AUTHOR'S NOTE

The service ranks, units and campaign deployments listed in the table of contents and the chapter headings reflect the time-line only for the stories depicted in this book. Some of those profiled are still serving in the military and have risen to higher ranks and have fought in additional conflicts. Those promotions and deployments are noted in their postscripts.

Unless otherwise noted, e-mail, social network messages and texts are presented as they were written by their senders.

I welcome your thoughts on the book as well as contributions of new stories from service members around the world that may be collected and published on a companion website. Please send them to me at things theycannotsay@gmail.com.

CONTENTS

Introduction: The Killer in Me   xvii

Prologue: Me and My PTSD   1

PART I

The Killing Business: What's It Like to Kill in War?

Chapter 1: Killing Up Close   25

    Corporal William Wold, U.S.M.C.

    3rd Battalion, 1st Marines

    The War in Iraq (2004)

Chapter 2: Pulling the Trigger   59

    Staff Sergeant Mikeal Auton, U.S. Army

    1st Battalion, 4th Infantry

    The War in Iraq (2004 and 2006)

PART II

**The Wounds of War: What's It Like to Be Shot,
Bombed or Burned in Combat?**

Chapter 3: Survivor's Guilt   77
   Lance Corporal James Sperry, U.S.M.C.
   3rd Battalion, 1st Marines
   The War in Iraq (2004)
Chapter 4: Someone's Not Listening   125
   Gunnery Sergeant Leonard Shelton, U.S.M.C.
   3rd Battalion, 5th Marines
   The Gulf War (1991)

Intermission: The Greatest Veneration: My Father's War   141

PART III

Things That Stain the Soul: What Can Never Be Forgotten?

Chapter 5: Dogs of War   153
   Specialist Joe Caley, U.S. Army
   1st Cavalry, 25th Infantry
   The War in Vietnam (1968–70)
Chapter 6: Hung on a Cross   165
   First Lieutenant Thomas Saal, U.S.M.C.
   3rd Battalion, 5th Marines
   The War in Vietnam (1967–68)

PART IV

**Deadly Honest Mistakes: What's It Like to Kill
Your Own Men or Civilians?**

Chapter 7: Unfriendly Fire 185

Specialist Michael "Casey" Ayala, U.S. Army

1st Battalion, 327th Infantry

The War in Iraq (2006)

Chapter 8: Making It Right 205

Captain Zachary Iscol, U.S.M.C.

3rd Battalion, 1st Marines

The War in Iraq (2003–05)

PART V

Moral Ambiguities: How Do You Know What's Right?

Chapter 9: Morris versus Mo 223

Colonel Morris Goins, U.S. Army

1st Battalion, 12th Cavalry

The War in Iraq (2006–08)

Chapter 10: The Quiet Soldier 233

Major Lior Tailer, Israel Defense Forces

609th Reserve Infantry Unit

The Wars in Lebanon (1989–90 and 2006)

Chapter 11: Into the Deep 255

Corporal Sebastiaan Schoonhoven, Royal Netherlands Army

11th Air Mobile Brigade

The Wars in Iraq and Afghanistan (2004 and 2006)

Contents

Epilogue: Deus Ex Machina 277

Acknowledgments 291

HOSPITAL PICTURES NO(1)

A soldier looked at
me with blue hawk-eyes
With kindly glances sorrow had made wise
And talked till all I'd ever read in books
Melted to ashes in his burning looks.

—Ivor Gurney, British soldier (World War I), poet, composer
From Ivor Gurney: *War's Embers*
(Sidgwick & Jackson Ltd., 1919)

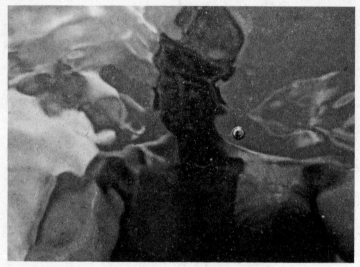
Self-portrait of the author, Lake Erie (2010)

INTRODUCTION

THE KILLER IN ME

In combat, inattention to detail can kill people.
—Karl Marlantes, *What It Is Like to Go to War*

I'M A journalist, not a soldier, but I've killed in combat. This is how I did it: I looked into the eyes of my victim as he begged for his life, lying before me covered in nothing but a ripped shirt, white underwear and his own dried blood, then I shrugged my shoulders, turned and walked away. I killed him with my indifference as much as the twenty-three 5.56 NATO rounds that tracked his spine as he tried to crawl away that few minutes or few hours after I left him in that mosque in south Fallujah.* I killed him without wielding a weapon, with-

---

* 5.56 x 45 mm NATO is a type of rifle ammunition developed in the United States originally for the M16 rifle but that also fits the M4, both issued to American soldiers and Marines during the wars in Iraq and Afghanistan. By contrast, for insurgents in Iraq and Taliban fighters in Afghanistan the primary combat rifle is the AK-47 rifle, which utilizes larger 7.62 x 39 mm rounds.

out being present and without knowing that I had killed him until three years later. It was only in that discovery, reading a heavily redacted Naval Criminal Investigative Service (NCIS) document about the incident, that I learned what I had done. Only in that moment, when the shaky, stacked soapboxes of my belief system came tumbling down, did the other face of war reveal itself to me fully. Until then, I had been happily chasing the dragon, my addiction to war, mostly immune to its consequences. No longer.

LIKE SO MANY ONCE-YOUNG journalists, I was a danger dilettante. In 1986, at the age of twenty-three, I traveled to Nicaragua as a passionate but clueless freelance reporter and photographer for an alternative newspaper to cover the U.S.-backed covert war against the leftist Sandinista government. I had $150 in my pocket, ten rolls of film in a quart-sized Ziploc bag, and a tenuous grasp of even rudimentary Spanish. I was looking for that shortcut to foreign-correspondent street cred, hoping to luck into a firefight, maybe get a bullet graze, but obviously understanding nothing. My research about conducting myself properly in a war zone consisted of watching Oliver Stone's *Salvador* three times. Once in country I headed to the infamous La Cita bar at Managua's Hotel Intercontinental and used my meager cash to buy bottles of the local *cerveza*, Victoria, for new friends staying at the hotel. After enough rounds, I convinced them to allow me to crash on the floor of their room. Once oriented in the capital, I used a credit card to rent a battered, old Toyota Sentra and drove north from Managua to the front lines with a Canadian military academy professor named Hal, who was kind enough to act as my interpreter and wise enough to realize that I was likely to get myself killed without his help.

I remember weaving through rutted mountain roads on Christmas Eve when two Sandinista soldiers walking along the road stopped us to ask for a ride. Their green jungle boonie caps dripped water from the cowboy-style brims as they loaded into the cramped backseat. I eyeballed the iconic curve of the banana mags jutting from their AK-47s and smelled the smoke of the campfire that they had earlier tried to warm themselves with on that cold, rainy evening. *"Feliz Navidad,"* we said to each other as I shifted into first, puttering into the cloud-shrouded darkness. In that moment, I felt I had transcended my small-town Ohio upbringing and had become part of the larger world, one that was comprised of excitement, danger and men with guns. While I never saw combat there, only its aftermath, villagers burying their dead following an attack, it was that first taste that would eventually help make war my heroin. I wanted to feel forever unburdened by the mundane realities of normal life, the way it was so perfectly illustrated by Kathryn Bigelow in her film *The Hurt Locker* when bomb tech First Sergeant William James is more disturbed by the sight of a well-stocked grocery store cereal aisle at home than of a massive roadside bomb engineered from daisy-chained 155 mm artillery shells in Iraq.

While it would be a decade before I got another real war "fix," this time as a producer for NBC News, my high returned easily and quite literally as my feet dangled outside the open door of a Navy Seahawk helicopter hovering over a U.S. destroyer in the waters of the Arabian Gulf, part of the U.S.-led post–Gulf War no-fly zone enforcement in Iraq. What kind of lucky bastard, I wondered, gets paid to be shuttled back and forth between battleships and aircraft carriers?

A few years after that I watched the start of the war in Kosovo, videotaping million-dollar Tomahawks launched at the Serbian capital of Belgrade from the deck of the guided-missile cruiser the USS *Philippine Sea*. The killing I "witnessed" up to and through Kosovo had always been at a distance. I saw weapons "release" but never their immediate impact. That changed for me during the wars in Afghanistan and Iraq.

KILLING TURNS EVERYTHING ON its head. Watching people being killed, especially those you know, is a memory that can't be erased. But actually doing the killing or being fully complicit in it is a lifelong sentence to contemplate the nature of one's own character, endlessly asking, "Am I good, or am I evil?" and slowly growing mad at the equivocation of this trick question whose answer is definitively yes.

When someone kills in war there's a psychological triage that occurs. The individual must find meaning in the act. Because killing is the ultimate refutation of our own humanity, there must be a justification, to prevent the mind from defaulting to the judgment of murderer.*

---

* Glenn Gray wrote in *The Warriors: Reflections on Men in Battle*, "The basic aim of a nation at war in establishing an image of the enemy is to distinguish as sharply as possible the act of killing from murder by making the former into

It's Private Joker trying to explain to the angry colonel in Stanley Kubrick's *Full Metal Jacket*, a 1987 film about the war in Vietnam, as to why he's wearing a peace symbol on his body armor while he's written "Born to Kill" on his helmet:

Private Joker: I think I was trying to suggest something about the duality of man, sir.

Colonel: The what?

Private Joker: The duality of man. The Jungian thing, sir.

In his book *What It Is Like to Go to War* former Vietnam War infantry officer and Rhodes scholar Karl Marlantes ruminates on the killing he did and the dying he watched on his deployment to that nation during America's ten-year conflict there. He learned, in the years after his service, that coming to terms with death is essential, but it has also become increasingly difficult in our age of modern warfare, where death, for many of those meting it out in Iraq and Afghanistan, has become an abstraction.

"Today a soldier can go out on patrol, kill someone or have one of his friends killed and call his girlfriend that night and talk about anything except what just happened. And if society itself tries to blur that as much as possible, by conscious

---

one deserving of all honor and praise." Gray enlisted in the U.S. Army as a private in 1941, the same day he received a doctorate in philosophy from Columbia University.

well-intended efforts to provide all the 'comforts of home' and modern transportation and communication, what chance does your average eighteen-year-old have of not being confused?"

Marlantes believes that grief and mourning for those a solider has killed as well as for the friends and comrades he's lost is key to the transformation that enables the warrior to find peace in the aftermath of battle. The absence of that grieving, which is often blocked by the numbing devices of alcohol, drugs, violence and empty sex, leave the warrior mired in the past, living in the midst of his "sins" and in endless judgment of himself, hopeless and without salvation. And with more than two million Americans having served in one or both of the decade-long conflicts in Iraq and Afghanistan, if society does not address that problem, it could have crippling social and economic consequences for the United States, including substance abuse, domestic violence, crime and the staggering medical and mental health care costs of providing for those veterans after their return and into old age.

"What is at stake is not just the psyche of each young fighter, but of our humanity," according to Marlantes. He continues:

> So ask the twenty-year-old combat veteran at the
> gas station how he felt about killing someone. His
> probable angry answer, if he's honest: "Not a fucking
> thing." Ask him when he's sixty and if he's not too
> drunk to answer, it might come out very differently,
> but only by luck of circumstance—who was there

executing a wounded, unarmed insurgent in a mosque (more on this later). The silence that met my inquiries became deafening.

But even with the soldiers and Marines whom I knew and in whom I had engendered a degree of trust, it was still a difficult process. Fear, I found, was the greatest barrier to the honest sharing of their wartime experiences: fear of reliving the experience, fear of judgment, fear of consequences, and fear, as psychologist Tick pointed out, of seeing oneself through a prism of innocence lost.

In many cases, after I contacted soldiers and Marines some would initially respond to an e-mail or two from me before slipping away. In other cases I actually began lengthy dialogues, before I lost them to concern about my intentions or the pain our conversations were reigniting rather than mitigating.

In one case, I interviewed a former soldier for two months. Let's call him Nate. Nate had been deeply scarred by burns following a roadside bomb incident in Iraq. He spoke with me openly and honestly until a conservative businessman and a financial patron of a program that assists wounded veterans mentioned that a journalist like me might not be Nate's best confessor. But eventually it was the rebellion of Nate's own subconscious that ended our dialogue. He had been in Iraq for a very short period of time before a roadside bomb blew up his convoy. Aside from that incident, he had almost no exposure to combat and its consequences. Additionally, while he remembers portions of the actual incident, because of the severity of his burns much of his early recovery was spent in a medically induced coma or so heavily drugged that he was barely aware of his surroundings. The upside to his post-trauma haze was an almost total lack of nightmares or other symptoms of PTSD (post-traumatic stress disorder). However, after I called him one final time to ask him to reconsider being part of the book he explained that our extended interviews were beginning to trigger an anxiety he had not felt before. He said he had begun to dream that his hand was on fire and that he couldn't put it out. Prior to our conversations, he said, he never dreamed of fire or the incident. At that moment, I realized the limitations of my knowledge. Sharing had helped me with my PTSD but perhaps there were, to use a medical term, contraindications for talk therapy as well. Dwelling too long or too deeply on past trauma forced someone like Nate to live repeatedly in that traumatic incident, rather than just visiting and moving past it. Now I was even more uncertain about the nature and direction of my work.

Another case that nearly derailed my convictions about the purpose and importance of this book concerned a soldier whom I'll call Henry. I embedded with Henry's unit at a dry, dirty and remote combat outpost in southern Afghanistan in the summer of 2006. There are usually two pronounced reactions when a solo journalist embeds in a platoon-sized infantry unit (thirty to forty individuals): some of the soldiers avoid you at every turn, assuming, sometimes correctly, that you're just as dangerous as any other battlefield booby trap; others seek you out, whether for your satellite phone, to bum some cigarettes or even just for conversation with someone from the outside. Henry was one of the seekers. We would sit on sandbags, smoke and talk in the heat of the Afghan summer night. Henry had a fascinating story, which he told me in great detail, about his life as a teenage gang member, a white kid who joined a set of the Crips on the East Coast. He was selling drugs at twelve and went to jail at fourteen for stabbing another gangbanger. He was heading for a bad end, he told me, until a sympathetic judge gave him a choice: prison or the Army. The choice was obvious and in the Army he had found a purpose for his unfocused energy and penchant for trouble. In boot camp, he told me, he learned discipline from a drill sergeant who had also been a gangbanger and saw through Henry's rebellious nature to his potential. He was thriving doing his job, making friends, until he was deployed to Iraq. There, Henry said, while in a patrol convoy, his best friend, a kid named Moreno, was killed by a roadside bomb. Henry blamed himself because he was the vehicle's turret gunner and should've seen the IED (improvised explosive device) before their vehicle hit it. Henry says he was devastated by Moreno's death and wanted payback. He told me that on the next patrol out, when a ten-year-old boy tried to throw a grenade at their convoy, he lit him up with the 50 cal. He didn't stop there. He then trained the weapon on the people lining the road, threading them with the muzzle of the large-caliber machine gun. When he stopped depressing the trigger, nine other people lay dead or dying. "Most of them," he told me softly, "had nothing to do with the attack, but fuck it, right? That's war." He shrugged.

As journalists we love these kinds of stories of trouble, redemption and then trouble again. Where would it lead, I wondered. Would Henry's experiences in the Army mess him up more than if he had simply gone to prison instead? When I returned home, I interviewed his mom and his girlfriend for the story. But as I began to dig deeper, I became concerned. While some of what he told me checked out, his troubled teens and stabbing another kid, there were also a lot of exaggerated details and some outright fabrications. Henry said that after the stabbing he was put in an adult prison, but in the state he's from it's against the law to hold a juvenile in an adult facility, regardless of their crime. Other more important elements also began to unravel. Most disturbingly, when I tried to find a record of his friend Moreno's death, I had no luck. I e-mailed Henry asking if he had mixed up the name or the year of the incident. No response. I checked the death records for the entire war and there was no record of this soldier, period. He existed, I discovered, only in Henry's world. It took months to get him to respond to me by e-mail. When he finally did, I asked him why he didn't just come clean with me, rather than wasting my time with this elaborate lie. He told me it was because he was afraid I would be angry with him. His response provided greater insight than the entire made-up story. Henry's need for attention and approval from an "authority figure" was so great, he felt he needed to lie to get it. I see it as a small, anecdotal signpost for the long-term consequences of sending eighteen- and nineteen-year-olds to do our dirty work in war. Infantry grunts, like Henry, are more often than not man-children who are asked to kill and die before their own sense of right and wrong has fully matured with years and non-war-related life experiences. For me, in writing this book, my time with Henry also reinforced the concept that a war story that sounds too sensational to be true likely is.

While the obstacles in gathering the material for this book and deciding what, if any, purpose it would serve were substantial, I decided that society as well as the soldiers would be better off for the *telling* and the *knowing*. I came to this conclusion after pondering my own experiences as well as a voluminous amount of clinical and anecdotal research about soldiers reentering their home societies. Most of it indicated the following: When a soldier decides not to share his life-defining moments in war with his wife, parents, children or community because of the accompanying guilt, shame, pain or any other valid reason, it increases the likelihood that he will feel more alienated from the society for which he was fighting, possibly to a debilitating degree. The alcohol, drugs and other self-medicating outlets for soldiers dealing with PTSD further isolate him from the normal comforts of a peacetime existence, work, family and friendships, and force him even deeper into the margins of society. Also, without the demythologized, demystified, authentic experiences of war being shared by those most directly involved in it, society itself will remain ignorant of the real practice of war, its costs and consequences.

A society "protected" from the reality of war can rewrite the narrative, shaping and forming it into something less terrible and costly by emphasizing only the heroism and triumphs rather than the dark, ugly deeds that occur with much greater frequency than we care to imagine or discuss.

More positively, the warrior who does share the descriptive and often disturbing narrative of his own war experiences reconnects himself to his community while simultaneously reminding them of the responsibilities that they also bear for his actions by sending him to fight and kill on their behalf. It's rarely an easy message to hear but it's essential to the positive evolution and enlightenment of the postconflict society. As Tick writes in *War and the Soul*, "Our society must accept responsibility for its warmaking. To the returning veterans, our leaders and people must say, 'you did this in our name and because you were subject to our orders, we lift the burden of your actions from you and take it onto our shoulders. We are responsible for you, for what you did and the consequences.'"

Stories are a way for societies to share in the burden of war. They provide knowledge necessary to better understand the warrior's experience and help them find meaning and sometimes forgiveness for their actions. Warriors, I've learned, become collateral damage too, killing a little of their own humanity every time they must pull the trigger, even though they do so at our bidding.

Tim O'Brien wrote so eloquently, in his classic Vietnam War novel *The Things They Carried*, "A true war story is never moral. It does not instruct, nor encourage virtue, nor suggest models of proper human behavior, nor restrain men from doing the things men have always done. If a story seems moral do not believe it."

My goal here is to try to tell the true war stories, not moral ones. The ones found here are entertaining, horrifying, brutally funny and banal, like so many other experiences. But because they involve war, they bring their own insistent drama that comes with the acts of fatal violence. The warriors brave enough to share them have already lived these stories. Now the communities they fought for need to honestly hear them, wherever they may lead.

As I mentioned, I sought out soldiers and Marines I knew and had reported on in the past, but I also found others, including those in the military service of other nations. I found them through veteran's groups, military associations and even medical and mental health professionals. This resulted in a broad base of interviews, providing a sampling of war experiences that ran the gamut from monstrous to mundane. Only a few made it into this book, primarily because I felt either the subjects were the most candid or their individual stories were the most instructive. Regardless, for all kind enough to share, the very act of their participation gave me hope that we may eventually see through the smoky glass of myth, parable and revisionism to something that resembles the *ground truth*.

On that point, these stories are recollections, oral histories from the perspectives of the men and women telling the stories. Like all who remember, they will remember imperfectly, with omissions and additions and perhaps lost players and parts. These are not after-action reports or official historical accounts, but the kind of stories that are true to their tellers and imbued with their own perspectives and even judgments. In fact, the primary sources in them are the individuals profiled. It was, after all, their perspective as combatants that I was seeking. They are difficult stories all, and I'm both grateful and hopeful that these acts of sharing will help bring these soldiers, and those who surround them, some peace. And as we see the war in Iraq ending and the Afghan war winding down, our communities will be filled with returning veterans carrying the physical and psychological burdens of their war experiences. We must hurry, using mostly our ears and hearts, to lighten the load.

THE THINGS THEY CANNOT SAY

The author sitting on an Iraqi antiaircraft missile (2003)

PROLOGUE
||||||||||||||||||||||||||||||||||||||||||||||

ME AND MY PTSD

Now the war is over, my war charms lie abandoned in
my bedroom, leaving me with death on my shoulder
and a monkey on my back. Peace seems to allow little
space for belief in destiny, fate, God or ghosts.
—Anthony Loyd, *My War Gone By, I Miss It So*

HERE'S WHAT happens when you come home from war:
the overload of excitement, intensity, absurdity, poi-
gnancy, foolishness, depth, danger, frivolity, importance and
delicious single-mindedness comes to a screeching halt. You've
been transformed through months of overstimulation fueled
by violence and the threat of it. I once believed this was a fate
only for the prosecutors of war and its victims, not for those
simply bearing witness. I was wrong. In war, there are no sidelines on which to sit.

War's most cunning trick, it seemed, was the war it seeded
within me. I wanted to cling to the concept of my own goodness, but the choices I had made during war seemed to indicate

something else entirely: a man who was at best oblivious and at worst heartless. It was that "Jungian thing" again, Private Joker pondering the "duality of man." For years, this confrontation for a dominant truth where none existed left me veering between wanting to be alone and never wanting to be alone, deliberate isolation and self-medicating social inebriation. Neither was a very good long-term companion.

But during my research I came across this quote by Virginia Woolf: "If you do not tell the truth about yourself you cannot tell it about other people." It resonated with me deeply. I knew I needed to tell the truth about myself to be able to do the same about others. But to do so, I first needed to learn the truth: was I a good man simply making bad choices, or had war simply stripped away that façade and revealed my dark character? I began my examination using a dry-erase board to sketch out the "case against me." Even as a schematic, the evidence for the latter appeared daunting. When I was done, it looked like this on the opposite page.

The case rests on three separate events that occurred in the last decade, in which I covered war almost exclusively. In general, these events represent the moral dilemmas that war poses for everyone exposed to it, even noncombatants like me. But specifically they are an ascending scale of defining moments representing the destructive and redemptive opportunities in the narrative of my own life. There were times when I wished and believed that the guilt from my choices would destroy me. There are times when I'm convinced that my life would have little significance without these events.

Regardless, they are mine and I must account for them. In their full explanations they may sound reasonable, but they sometimes feel like the popgun rantings of a soul in full disequilibrium.

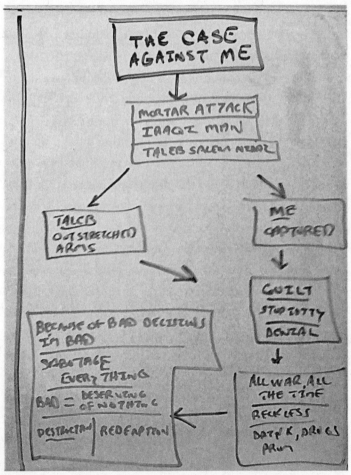

"The Case Against Me" schematic on dry-erase board

Number One starts in northern Afghanistan with a simple hesitation. It's October 2001 on a hill in an area near the border with Tajikistan known as Pul-i-Khomri. It's a place in which deep trench lines, reminiscent of World War I, separate the ruling Afghan Taliban forces from the Northern Alliance fighters seeking to oust them. The two sides are casually tossing mortars back and forth, taunting each other on the same radio frequency as if they were engaged in nothing more deadly than a backyard game of badminton. I'm on a mound of dirt topped with a Russian-made T-62 tank left over from the Soviet invasion, with a few journalist colleagues. We're talking and laughing at the absurdity of it all until we hear a crack in the distance. The tank commander is peering at the Taliban lines through my spotting scope, which I bought for a few dollars at a street market in the Uzbek capital of Tashkent two weeks back on my way into Afghanistan. Through my video camera's viewfinder, I watch him drop the scope and dive behind the tank. The ground shakes as the mortar round explodes thirty feet behind us. Bounding shrapnel tears into the thigh and glutes of a producer for *National Geographic* who's standing on my left, just inches away from me. He goes down. "I'm hit, I'm hit," he says, grabbing his leg in pain. I've been recording video the entire time, including the last shell impact. I swing my camera over to the producer and the blood is now seeping through his hands as he holds them against the wounds. It's dramatic and rare footage, a seldom-captured incoming round and its casualty, the ultimate cause and effect. I know our news audience does not see this kind of thing very often. It's remarkable and, in my mind, instructive in an obvious way. This is what really happens when hard metal meets soft flesh. I shout to the others to take cover on the other side of the tank since the Taliban will discover through their own spotting scopes that they've got this site dialed in. But this is just the beginning of my dilemma. As a journalist I don't want to stop shooting, even while the producer bleeds. If the shrapnel has penetrated his leg's femoral artery, one of the body's largest, he will bleed out in less than four minutes unless something is done. I continue to shoot. He even prompts his own videographer, whose camera missed everything: "Hey, shoot this," he says, still holding his leg. I feel the strange tug of something at my shirttail while I continue to roll. It's light but insistent, probably just my conscience. I want to ignore it, but finally and with reluctance, I put the camera on the dirt next to the wounded producer but leave it on record. My own adrenaline is pumping as I begin to realize that I'm lucky to be alive myself, given the producer's proximity to me. In fact, if he hadn't been standing where he was to absorb the flying shards of metal, I might be the one bleeding now instead. "Give me the fucking scarf," I say, amped by adrenaline. Pulling it from his neck, I wind it around his thigh several times and then tie it off tightly above the bleed. I pick up the camera when I'm done, point it at him and ask how it feels to have been hit with a mortar round. "It's like a tornado that has torn through my leg," he says. It's only later in recounting the story that I realize, I didn't choose him over the shot. I chose both. He will live and even bask in some media attention in the immediate aftermath, but I wonder if the same would be true if the shrapnel had hit the artery and I still hesitated before wrapping the wound to make sure I got my shot.

In the case against me, Number Two begins with this question: "Are you going to videotape me if I shoot him?" It's November 2004. I'm following two Marines through the streets of Fallujah during the first day of the ground offensive to take back the city from insurgents. It's called Operation Phantom Fury, but so far, with the exception of a few bodies here and there, there don't seem to be many insurgents left. But as we come into an opening between buildings, I see an older Iraqi man lying on the ground, a close-cropped white beard in stark contrast to the maroon stream of blood running in a little channel from his head to the curb. His shirt is open, exposing a white T-shirt underneath and a chest that is rising and falling in what seem to be agonal breaths, likely his last. His right hand rests on his chest, while the left arm is bent at the elbow and pointing up, the hand cupped open, weirdly reminiscent of the queen of England's wave. I move closer to see the extent of his injuries but reel back when I see that the right side of his head is missing. While he looked complete from a distance, a Marine sniper had fired a round through his eyeball, taking much of his skull and brain through the exit wound in the back. Yet, it seems so oddly clean, almost surgical. After I walk back over to the Marines, one of them asks me the question, "Are you going to videotape me if I shoot him?" I don't think there's any malice behind the question. It's a mercy killing, I'm nearly certain. I respond almost automatically: "Of course I am, that's my job," I say, but as the words come out of my mouth, I'm wondering why I can't just let the Marine finish the job without videotaping it. Doubtless, the man is going to die. Why not let it be without more suffering? The Marine shrugs, tells the other something along the lines of it's not worth the risk of getting into trouble—"The guy's going to die anyway." The two of them walk on and leave me alone with the Iraqi man with half a head missing. I look at him. He's still breathing, still bleeding. What's left of his life is in my hands now. I wonder if this is the worst way to die, alone with no one who can even understand your last words, if you have any. I wonder if I should've let the Marine shoot him. I don't know if he's suffering terribly or if that sniper's bullet removed any sense of pain or awareness along with that part of his head. I wonder how I became the final arbiter of the last moments of his existence. I look at him again and realize we are alone in this place together. The Marines are gone; there's no one else around. This Iraqi man, dressed in civilian clothes, most likely in his mid to late fifties, has no weapon by his side and perhaps never did. He is almost certainly someone's father, maybe even a grandfather, but there's no one around him now, only me. He will die lying on the ground as a stranger holding a video camera looks over him. But I can't let that happen. It's just not right. So here is what I do instead: I walk away. I follow the path of the Marines and let him breathe his last breath alone in the street. The twinge of guilt I felt disappeared once the shooting started again, just around the corner. I left the half-headed man behind . . . or so I thought.

That should be enough, but it's not. Number Three is the most egregious thing I have ever done in my life: I walked away again, but this time from a man very much alive and pleading with me to help him. When I left the room he was murdered.

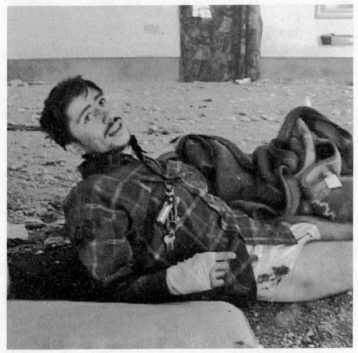

Taleb Salem Nidal, the man who was murdered after I failed to help him

Taleb Salem Nidal was one of five wounded Iraqi insurgents who had been captured by U.S. Marines after a confused engagement in a Fallujah mosque. The fighting took place during one of the biggest and bloodiest American-led military operations since the Vietnam War, Operation Phantom Fury. In November 2004, more than thirteen thousand American, British and Iraqi government troops took up positions north of the city, poised to push south, flushing out and killing the insurgents who had controlled Fallujah for months. Nidal was holed up with more than a dozen other fighters inside a mosque in south Fallujah. A week into the battle, Marines reached the mosque and after taking fire, hit back hard. (The early stages of this engagement are detailed in chapter 1.) When the smoke finally cleared, ten of the insurgents were dead and five injured.

Nidal was one of the lucky ones. He had been only slightly wounded in the leg. He was captured after the Marines took the mosque and was given medical treatment from Navy corpsmen along with the other insurgents. The Marine battalion commander assured me the wounded Iraqi prisoners were going to be transported back to field headquarters for further treatment and interrogation. But whether it was a lie or just an oversight in the heat of a furious battle, it never happened. Nidal and the other four survivors were left in the mosque overnight disarmed, untended and unguarded along with the stinking corpses of their ten dead comrades partially stuffed into American body bags. The next day a Marine lance corporal from the same battalion went back into the mosque and shot all of the wounded men again, *except* Taleb Salem Nidal, who covered himself with a blanket and was likely considered one of the dead. It's unclear whether this Marine knew that these insurgents had been wounded and captured the day before, but he had to have some idea of the earlier engagement with the body bags still littering the mosque floor and the fact that the survivors were unarmed and sporting fresh bandages.

According to his own deposition in a Naval Criminal Investigative Service (NCIS) report, the Marine says he began shooting the injured Iraqis first with his M16 rifle, but when it jammed, he used his Beretta M9 pistol. I remember hearing the rounds while I waited outside the mosque. They were unhurried, with several-second intervals in between, the methodical nature of someone taking aim and shooting targets, rather than shots fired in fear or anger. Stranger and even more disturbing was what happened next. I entered the mosque with another Marine fireteam shortly after hearing the shots inside. I was surprised to see the bodies still in the mosque and even more surprised to see that four of the five wounded and captured insurgents who were supposed to be transported back to battalion headquarters were now either dead or dying from fresh gunshot wounds. Automatically, I began to document the scene, videotaping the dying men lying against the mosque's far wall. As I did, I saw in the corner of my frame a Marine (the same Marine, I would learn later from the NCIS reports, who had shot the captured insurgents). I tilted up slightly as I heard him say of one of the wounded men he had just shot before I entered the mosque, *"He's fucking faking he's dead— he's faking he's fucking dead."*

Then I watched through my viewfinder as he raised his M16 and fired one final round into the man. It was an execution shot from point-blank range, blowing his brains out against the back wall of the mosque in which he had been slumped. I saw the proverbial pink mist that anyone who's ever witnessed a headshot claims to have seen. For a moment it mingled with the particles of dust riding the sunbeam from a mosque window to the rubble-strewn floor.

"He's dead now," another Marine said, uttering a statement so profoundly redundant that it seemed simply an exclamation point to the act. Then the Marine spun on his heel and walked away, as if he had done nothing more than dispatch a rabid dog. In a killing such as this, there's a temporary vacuum in the air that sucks the breath out of anyone watching. I could feel my stomach rise to my throat. I knew that in this moment everything had changed. I had stumbled into a moral limbo where there existed the slippery concept that even in the mayhem of war, there were rules about killing. As technology was my witness, I had unwittingly become part of this unresolved conversation simply by pushing the red button on my camera.

When I confronted the Marine and asked him why he shot the man who had been wounded yesterday, he simply said, "I didn't know, sir, I didn't know." He walked out with the other Marines and left me alone with Taleb Salem Nidal, who had pulled his blanket down and revealed his leg wound and the underpants he was wearing, his only clothing besides his shirt. He began talking to me in Arabic, asking me to help him. I watched him through my viewfinder, as I had the Iraqi who had been executed just moments before. Nidal's arms were outstretched, pleading. I told him I didn't speak Arabic, though the look on his face was clearly that of a man who knew he was in great danger, having just witnessed his wounded friends all being shot a second or third time. He fell back on his elbows, resigned, noting by my lack of expression that I would do nothing for him. He was right. I turned away from him as he lay on the floor, in his dirty white underwear, chunks of concrete and debris surrounding him.

I walked out of the mosque angered by the murder that I had just witnessed but somehow oblivious that Nidal could be next. I wanted to find the battalion commander and show him the videotape. Who was to blame? Was the Marine acting on his own or following orders not to leave anyone alive behind their lines of advance?* Ultimately it didn't matter. NBC and I decided to self-censor the report and not show the actual shooting, assuming it might be too inflammatory.† Our actions botched the story. By agreeing to censor the video, we kept important information from being part of the critical public discourse during a time of war. I had failed in my duty as a journalist and that failure haunted me for years.

I went back to reporting on war, but I never stopped thinking about what had happened in that Fallujah mosque. Wanting some kind of closure, I filed a Freedom of Information Act request with the U.S. government, desperate to get any other

---

* During my research, I discovered that on at least two other occasions Iraqi prisoners were executed during Operation Phantom Fury.

† I later independently released the entire raw video of the mosque shooting on NPR's website.

details. In 2007, three years after the mosque shooting, the full report of the Naval Criminal Investigative Service arrived in my mailbox. It was the size of a Manhattan telephone book and heavily redacted (sections blacked out for privacy protection of individuals named in the case and purportedly for other national security concerns). I took a deep breath and dug in, uncertain what I would find. It took me only twenty minutes and what I read made my knees buckle.

Taleb Salem Nidal, the wounded Iraqi who had been under the blanket and had tried to talk with me after the shooting, was himself murdered sometime after I left the mosque. His autopsy report detailed that his death was the result of the twenty-three bullet rounds fired into his back. When I bumbled out of the mosque with my videotape to seek justice for one summary execution, I had set the stage for another by ignoring the obvious probability that it would happen again. And it did. Had I simply walked Nidal out of the mosque, he might've lived. He had been the only witness besides me. Left alone in the aftermath, he never had a chance. To this day, I can't begin to fathom how I could have been so stupid. I never intended to get him killed, but with even a sliver more compassion in place of my "righteous" anger I might have saved him. His death is the pinnacle in the case against me. I have carried its burden ever since and in all but the last year or so, I've compounded the sin by bearing it with a complete and utter lack of grace.

My post-traumatic stress didn't begin with the realization of that final crime, but it certainly took me pro. I had indulged in all kinds of bad behavior throughout my "war career." Drinking, recreational drugs and empty sexual encounters were part of my damaged-foreign-correspondent repertoire. According to the former VA psychiatrist Jonathan Shay in his second book on post-traumatic stress, *Odysseus in America: Combat Trauma and the Trials of Homecoming*, veterans and I had a lot in common. "Veterans use many strategies to numb their pain, to silence the nightmares, to quell guilt," he wrote. "Chemicals are only one such strategy, danger seeking is another, workaholism is another, sexaholism another still—and it is not an exaggeration to see it all."

As soon as I felt the tinglings of discomfort brought on by trigger sounds of choppers, terrain resembling Iraq or Afghanistan or even seeing people in Islamic dress, I would find myself mucking into the past and waist-deep in melancholy, either disturbed by the recollections of being there or disturbed by the fact that I wasn't there. Either way, I delivered my anesthetics quickly and without guilt, knowing from books and movies that this was the way you dealt with the memories of war. Despite my deepening problems of addiction and abuse, I resisted any counseling or therapy, considering it a sign of weakness, for those who couldn't cope. But the truth was I hadn't been coping at all. My answer to the war within myself was to spend more time at war. I responded to the initial personal impact of the mosque shooting (before learning about the murder of Nidal) not with contemplation but with more conflict. If I had a theme song it would've been Elvis Presley singing "A little less conversation . . . a little more action." I joined the giant Internet portal Yahoo! with the idea for a website called Kevin Sites in the Hot Zone, a project in which I would travel alone and report on every major war on the planet in one year.

The Hot Zone simultaneously added to my collection of nightmares while helping me to contain them for another year and a half. I was in a new relationship, but that one also began to quickly unravel when I got back from my year at war and began writing *In the Hot Zone*, my memoir of that journey. It was then, in doing the research for that book, that I discovered the fate of Taleb Salem Nidal.

With that realization, I began a scorched-earth campaign that covered thousands of miles and another five years. No family member, no friend, no relationship was safe from my alternating anger and sullen isolation, though I did a formidable job of hiding both for long stretches, behind constant activity and bottomless martinis. I wrote and gave speeches touching the surface of my experiences, mistakes and realizations, but seldom prying deeper, not fully understanding the seismic shift they had set in motion in my psyche. I was just treading water, filling the void with kinetic energy and alcohol. I studied and earned certification as an emergency medical technician, I learned to rock-climb, I went on an expedition across Tanzania and climbed Mount Kilimanjaro. At the time, I was with a woman eighteen years younger than me who was both bewildered and overwhelmed by the self-hatred that began to manifest as nearly total physical and emotional withdrawal. When that relationship ended, I was really on my own to do what I wanted with no pretense of obligation to anyone but myself.

I decided to flee to a beautiful but remote wind-blown rock north of Venezuela, the Dutch Antilles island of Bonaire. There I would trade my car for a bicycle, my camera for a mask and fins, and drop off the radar to work in a local scuba shop.

But in the spring of 2009, a week before leaving for Bonaire, I learned that I had been awarded a prestigious yearlong Nieman Fellowship for journalism at Harvard starting in September. I might have been able to escape journalism for a few months, but not forever. The Nieman was a competitive award that paid twelve domestic and twelve international fellows a stipend of $60,000 for the privilege of being in residence at Harvard University for nine months and doing nothing more than auditing classes in any particular subject that caught their fancy, from undergraduate history courses to medical school dissection labs. The initial idea was to give journalists a more well-rounded education—a Renaissance year. The only thing the Nieman Foundation asked of you was that you be engaged with the university and your colleagues. If there was a caveat, it was a minor one: while they did not forbid you to use the year to work on book projects, they discouraged it as an interference to the atmosphere of academic and collegial immersion. But after leaving Yahoo! News in 2008 I was back in the freelance world, which meant I couldn't afford to let a paid year go by without taking advantage of it. I had to write this book. And in that well-intentioned effort, I had no idea how badly I would squander this gift.

It began with my housing choice, which was to live in one of the undergraduate "River Houses" called Dunster, which kept a furnished, two-bedroom apartment open for Nieman Fellows each year. Usually international students grabbed the space, but I took it after being told how difficult it would be to find a spot in the high-priced Cambridge apartment market. The following August, I settled into the dark, cold and cavernous two-bedroom on the ground floor and began to research and plot out this book. Often that took place with a glass of red wine in one hand and a cigarette in the other. Harvard rules, however, forbid smoking anywhere on campus within twenty feet of a university building. That, I surmised, would make it impossible to reach my keyboard. Instead, I set my chair by the window and blew the offending smoke outside. Unfortunately it traveled up to the sensitive nose of some undergrad who ratted me out. After I ignored the e-mails from the resident assistant in my section of the building, the RA went to the house master, who was usually a tenured professor, and their family who lived in a house next to the residence hall. In this case it was a professor of business and his wife. They were a Mormon couple not particularly impressed by my behavior. Soon I was sitting in front of Bob Giles, then the grandfatherly curator of the Nieman Foundation, who reminded me in a polite but firm way that while I was living in a dorm for undergraduates, I didn't have to act like one. I was a forty-seven-year-old man getting reprimanded for smoking at school. It was definitely time to move. Dunster House had been bad for my self-esteem anyway, considering that if I had just worn a maroon polo shirt, like the building maintenance men, I would've likely been mistaken for one since they were so much closer to my age.

I moved out and rented a studio apartment overlooking Cambridge Common, where George Washington first took command of the Continental Army. It was on the second floor and full of light and character. My bed wedged perfectly into a small alcove, allowing me to lie on it and read while watching over the seasons, first the leaves, then the rain and finally the snow falling to the ground below. It was perfect. This would be the place where I would fight my own revolution, the battle against myself. But almost immediately, I began to lose. I frequently skipped my classes and social outings with fellow Niemans under the pressure of getting work done on the book. But as I stared at my computer screen transcribing notes from an interview with a soldier or Marine, the crushing weight of the stories that they shared with me often set off the anger and despair lodged in my own unresolved narrative. Thinking about their stories forced me to think of my own and the choices I had made in war. I countered these unpleasant thoughts by lying on my back on the hardwood floor next to my fireplace, drinking shots of whiskey and smoking cigarette after cigarette, exhaling the smoke into my chimney, reminding me of the indigenous people I once reported on from Chiapas, Mexico, who drank Coca-Cola and burped skyward, believing it to be a prayer to God. My God, I believed, had become bored with my prayers and my stories.

It was not inertia or laziness that kept me from making progress on the book. It was the shock of finally being forced to continually confront the psychological detritus of my years at war. Being in a safe environment where I was encouraged to be introspective loosed the lid of my jack-in-the-box issues. Whatever control I thought I had, I quickly lost in the repeated examination and judgment of my past. I saw the face of Taleb Salem Nidal everywhere from my dreams to the soot stains on the fireplace.

I was also having so much trouble cornering sources and getting them to talk to me that I began to think the whole project was futile. Writing became so difficult that at first I could grind out a page or two before going for a cigarette, then it would become a paragraph or two, eventually a sentence and then, after staring at the screen long enough with nothing coming out, I would start drinking again, trying to trick myself into believing it would loosen my brain and the words would come. They rarely did. I became so frustrated that I convinced myself that the problem wasn't post-traumatic stress but attention deficit disorder. I knew the drug Adderall was commonly prescribed for ADD, but I also knew that college students used it illicitly to help them focus, study harder and stay up longer. I finally got the courage to ask my doctor to prescribe it for me as a test. He did so, reluctantly.

The first time I took it, I used the proper dosage of two ten-milligram pills. It gave me a jittery sensation, but also, I believed, the ability to better concentrate. In a few days I had written more than I had in weeks. For a moment, I felt I had found my cure. But when it wore off, I was exhausted. Like cocaine, Adderall puts your whole nervous system on overdrive. I started exceeding the proper dosage by twice or sometimes three times the amount. I would sit down at my computer, type a few lines but then become too jittery to work. I needed a drink to cut the effect and then a cigarette with the drink. Soon I was on the floor of my apartment again instead of at my laptop, blowing billows of smoke up at my chimney that drifted, I imagined, down to the common, mingling with the ghosts of Washington and his army preparing to lay siege to Boston. After this brief surge of pharmaceutical-induced hope, my writing again hit a wall.

But while I couldn't write, I could think, and Taleb Salem Nidal was never far from my thoughts. In my head, I would play back the video I shot of him, see the resignation on his face and hear his voice as I walked away. Sometimes when I was fully immersed in the Mardi Gras of my own self-destruction, I would try to talk to people about what I had done, and the combination of my desperate earnestness and slurring words made the dark tale even more unpalatable and almost impossible to understand. The burden remained mine alone.

Once, after a night of heavy drinking, I stood staring up at a lamppost, wondering why I shouldn't just unsheathe my belt, loop it over my neck and tie the other end to the base of the light. It was, I thought, simple math—a life for a life. If not that night, soon I would have to make a choice.

PART I

The Killing Business

What's It Like to Kill in War?

PHANTOM NOISE

There is this ringing hum   this
bullet-borne language   ringing
shell-fall and static this   late-night
ringing of threadwork and carpet   ringing
hiss and steam   this wing-beat
of rotors and tanks   broken
bodies ringing in steel   humming these
voices of dust   these years ringing
rifles in Babylon   rifles in Sumer
ringing these children their gravestones
and candy   their limbs gone missing   their
static-borne television   their ringing
this eardrum   this rifled symphonic   this
ringing of midnight in gunpowder and oil this
brake pad gone useless   this muzzle-flash singing   this
threading of bullets in muscle and bone   this ringing
hum   this ringing hum   this
ringing

     —Brian Turner, U.S. soldier (Iraq and Bosnia),
           writer-poet, educator[*]

[*] "Phantom Noise" from *Phantom Noise*. Copyright © by Brian Turner. Reprinted with the permission of The Permissions Company, Inc., on behalf of Alice James Books, www.alicejamesbooks.org.

Corporal William Wold, U.S.M.C.
3rd Battalion, 1st Marines
The War in Iraq (2004)

CHAPTER 1

KILLING UP CLOSE

I'll never tell her what things I did here.
I'll never tell anybody.

I MAGINE YOU are a Marine ordered to clear a building during one of the bloodiest battles of a particularly brutal and dirty war. Anything could be waiting for you inside: mines, booby traps, goats, women, children . . . or fully armed enemy fighters. Once you discover what's on the other side of the wall, you will have to make a decision in a fraction of a second about whether you need to pull the trigger or not. The marvels of modern weaponry—robot drones, guided cruise missiles and even small arms that have great accuracy over long distances—have made this kind of close-quarters combat mightily rare and mostly unnecessary. But this day, for Corporal Willy Wold, is one of the exceptions. When I see him, he's standing in front of a wall outside a mosque in Fallujah and firmly in the almost manic-rapturous throes of a full-tilt adrenaline dump, the kind you get when you come face-to-face with your enemies and kill half a dozen of them before they can kill you.

Only about forty minutes ago, his fireteam had entered the mosque in south Fallujah from which insurgents had been shooting. At one point during this war American military leadership had decided not to attack mosques, even if insurgents were fighting from inside. The public-relations blowback of destroying a Muslim holy place undoubtedly created more insurgents instead of fewer. But this unofficial policy also gave rise to what American military strategist and historian Edward Luttwak calls the "paradoxical strategy of war," which, in very simplified terms, proffers that regardless of the soundness of your strategic thinking on the battlefield, your enemy will quickly adapt and use your practices against you. Because the Americans weren't attacking mosques, insurgents routinely fought from them, even using their towering minarets as sniper nests. Frustrated, American generals decided before Operation Phantom Fury, a major offensive to drive insurgents from Fallujah, that the restraints were coming off and if insurgents holed up in a mosques, those mosques were coming down.*

---

* Operation Vigilant Resolve, or the First Battle of Fallujah, began in early April 2004 in retaliation after four Blackwater American security contractors were killed and their bodies burned on a bridge in Fallujah that March. It ended less than a month later with a cease-fire that handed over security responsibilities in Fallujah to a force of Iraqi Sunnis known as the Fallujah Brigade. The brigade was supposedly allied with the American military and the Iraqi government but soon switched sides, joining the insurgents, turning over weapons to them or

This mosque that Willy Wold entered would be an example of that new policy. When Marines took fire from it, they responded by blasting holes through the walls with high-explosive rounds fired through the 120 mm main guns of their M1A1 Abrams tanks. Soon after, a squad of Marines led by Lance Corporal Patrick O'Brien entered the mosque. They found one dead and five wounded insurgents (the same mentioned in the prologue), likely the result of the tank's rounds.

The wounded Iraqis inside the main hall surrendered without a fight, slumped against the back wall bleeding and broken. But there was another room that hadn't been checked out yet. O'Brien ordered Wold and his three-man fireteam to stack on it (SWAT-style) and make sure it was clear.

Wold did as he was told and on his signal, his men loaded into the room, one sweeping to the right with his rifle muzzle, the other to the left and Wold up the middle, like the linebacker he was in high school. They found nothing initially, but there was another doorway.

The first Marine entered and his pupils nearly popped trying to take in what was before him inside: nine armed insurgents, all bearded and ranging in age from midtwen-

---

both. Operation Phantom Fury, or the Second Battle of Fallujah, was about correcting that mistake. With more than thirteen thousand American, British and Iraqi government troops, Fallujah was brought under military control in forty-five days. It was the bloodiest battle of the War in Iraq, with as many as fifteen hundred insurgents killed and more than a hundred coalition troops. Eight hundred civilians were also estimated to have died.

ties to midthirties. Some wore shirts and trousers, the others traditional dishdashas, which the American troops derisively referred to as "man dresses." They were armed with AKs and RPG launchers, but at that moment of recognition, no one fired. There was the momentary "holy shit" pause, followed by the pulse wave of fear that violence is imminent. Wold yelled, "Shoot him," to the first Marine, who blasted the man in front of him. Pushing in, Wold fired into the group as well while his other Marine covered him on the left, putting rounds into the mass of men, who were close enough to hug. When the bodies had all dropped, Wold and his team had fired more than three dozen rounds total. The Marines took a breath, knowing they had dodged their own death by the smallest of margins. They pushed away the insurgents' weapons and did their dead checks, nudging the bodies in the groin and other sensitive spots with their boots or rifle barrels. If anyone was still alive it would have been impossible not to flinch. The Marines picked up the fallen weapons and stacked them outside at the front entrance of the mosque.

Later, I watched as the squad reluctantly carried the bodies to the main hall of the mosque, where the wounded insurgents lay. On the bodies of the dead, I could see the precision of the Marines' shots, controlled bursts to heads and center mass, just as they were trained to do. A piece of brain matter fell from the head of one of the insurgents and a Marine used a piece of wood to scoot it across the floor, back toward its owner. There were some small fist-bumps and bro-hugs amongst the

Marines in the aftermath, but the lumps of lifeless bodies sucked up any sense of jubilation in this victory. It's one thing to kill your enemies in battle; it's quite another to have to hoist their bullet-ridden bodies, by wrists or ankles or waistbands, and drop them in a pile, dead eyes open, breathless mouths agape, the stench of their soiled clothes mixed with the sulfur smell of cordite still thick in the air. While others dragged the corpses toward unrolled black body bags, Wold shuffled around them, surveying the destruction, not sure what he was supposed to be feeling.

Wold shook his head ever so slightly while the brigade commander, Lieutenant Colonel William Buhl, snapped his profile with a silver point-and-shoot camera, the victor in the aftermath. As the Marines continued their unpleasant work, fitting the dead two to a body bag, the wounded insurgents tried to avert their gaze, fearful they might yet share the same fate as their comrades. They wouldn't on that day. Instead they were bandaged by Navy corpsmen accompanying the Marines and given water. The wounded included an old man in his late fifties or early sixties with a red kaffiyeh wrapped around his head; a stocky man, maybe thirty-five, in a gray dishdasha; a young man with a mustache in his late twenties, wearing only a shirt and his underwear, his wounded leg exposed (Taleb Salem Nidal, discussed in the prologue); and finally, a man in his early thirties with multiple wounds to the neck, arms and torso, wearing the shreds of an Iraqi police uniform, dark slacks and a light blue shirt. Despite his wounds and dirty, tattered clothes, he had a strong and handsome face, a neatly trimmed mustache and a firm jaw. Of all of the wounded men, he seemed to me the most stoic, betraying neither his fear nor his suffering.*

When I saw Wold on the street outside the mosque afterward, these were his first words to me as I watched him through my video camera viewfinder:

"It was a fucking small room, dude. It was fucking small!" He shook his head. "Thirty-five fucking rounds. I was fucking scared, dude. I fucking grabbed my nuts." Then he did, with one hand, and let out a big "Ohhh!"

"Tell me what you saw," I said to him. He shook his head again in disbelief.

"I was told to go in the room," he said, "and my first Marine went in . . . he saw a guy with an AK, I told him to shoot the guy, then I shot the six guys on the left . . . and my other Marine shot two other guys."

A flood of questions filled my mind. I wanted to understand where the men were standing, the expressions on their faces, what it felt like to pull the trigger at such a short distance.

---

* His name, I discovered from Naval Criminal Investigation Service reports, was Farhan Abd Mekelf, and according to the identification found on his body, he was an Iraqi policeman. He was the insurgent executed at point-blank range by a Marine lance corporal in front of my video camera the day *after* Wold's fire-team first entered the mosque and confronted the room full of armed insurgents. I was asked a few days later after his shooting by an NCIS investigator to identify him inside his body bag at a storage building at a U.S. military base. I could tell it was him, even though his face was crumpled and collapsed into itself, reminding me of a rubber Halloween mask with a tuft of black hair on top.

How did their bodies, faces change? Did they simply crumple where they stood or did they fly back as if yanked by an invisible rope like what happens in the movies? All these questions, but none found words. "Tell me what you saw," I blurted out again. Here was where curiosity and morbidity intersected, became indistinguishable.

"All I saw was guns pointed at me"—he shook his head again—"so it was just instinct to blare 'em. I gotta go," he said, moving toward the sound of shouting and confusion.

I followed Wold down the street, where he learned that a friend of his had just been wounded. The single attacker vaulted over a wall. Wold took a fireteam inside the courtyard in pursuit, his adrenaline rush now fueling his anger.

"Get in that motherfucker and kill his ass," he shouted as his team kicked in a metal gate. I followed them in, videotaping everything. They fired bursts into both buildings inside the courtyard. Nothing. Wold tossed a grenade through the space between the buildings, yelling, "Frag out," as they piled outside for cover behind the courtyard wall. When there was no detonation, he sent another one of his guys in with another grenade. This one blew, its explosion muffled by the cinder blocks of the buildings. They rushed back into the courtyard, clearing the buildings as they had done earlier in the mosque, but this time there was no one pointing guns at them. In fact, there was no one at all. They came back frustrated and disappointed to the armored personnel carrier where the wounded Marine was being treated. Wold wanted blood for blood, but that would have to wait.

When I caught up with him again it was nearly dusk and his adrenaline had dipped only slightly. It was clear that Wold was still processing the life-and-death encounter he'd just had. His mind was spinning and he didn't want to keep all his thoughts to himself. Over the next thirty minutes he dropped his guard and spoke with brutal honesty, perhaps instinctively realizing how important it was for me and others to understand that he was once just a normal young man, a boy really, who went to prom and played football in high school, but now here in Iraq he'd just added six to the number of lives he'd had to take. We talked, through the sound of machine guns, tanks and even an air strike. Our conversation was interrupted only by his movement and commands to his other Marines. It continued until dark and I rolled with my infrared light until the squad leader screamed at me to turn it off. This is the transcript of our videotaped conversation. (Watch this exchange and other footage of Corporal William Wold; the actual interview begins at 22.55: https://www.youtube.com/watch?v=Yfrr3kxzJtU&feature=plcp.)

FRIDAY, NOVEMBER 12, 2004

William Christopher Wold (WW): It gets dark and we're gonna be hurtin'.

Kevin Sites (KS): Did you see what happened over there?

WW: Yeah, well, one of the other NCOs was just walkin' by Danger. We had security. One of these fuckin' shitheads just jumped out and fuckin' shot him a bunch of times. And then ran and jumped over a fuckin' wall and we couldn't get his ass. He got shot five or six times. The sappy plate stopped most of the rounds. One went right into his fuckin' . . . one went into his neck and the other one went into his arm.

KS: What's your name, man?

WW: What's that?

KS: What's your name?

WW: Willy.

KS: Willy, what's your last name?

WW: Wold. Corporal Wold.

KS: Wold? How do you spell that?

WW: W-O-L-D. Only got six months left, man. I just wanna get the fuck out of this place. Get outta my corps.

KS: Outta the Marine Corps, too?

WW: Yeah. I'm done. I'll be a sergeant pretty soon and then I'm gonna get out.

KS: How many years do you have?

WW: I've been in three and a half.

KS: How old are you?

WW: I just turned twenty-one.

KS: Where are you from?

WW: Washington State.

KS: The stuff you've seen during this war . . .

WW: What's that?

KS: The stuff you've seen during this war, has it changed you?

WW: I . . . you gotta say that again.

KS: The stuff that you've had to see in this war, and do, has it changed you?

WW: Yeah. A lot. I'm real young. I joined the Marine Corps at seventeen. I guarded the president of the United States for two and a half years and then I came out here. It's changed me a lot.*

KS: How so?

WW: It just changes your aspect on life. You don't take a lot of shit for granted that you used to.

KS: You had to shoot some guys today.

WW: Yeah.

KS: Was that hard to do?

WW: No. I don't have a problem shootin' shitheads.

KS: Have you had to do it before this?

WW: Yeah. I shot twelve guys since I've been here.

KS: Twelve guys and you just turned twenty-one?

WW: What's that?

KS: Twelve guys and you've just turned twenty-one?

WW: [*Laughs*] Yeah. I get out at twenty-one. I came in at seventeen. I graduated high school a year early to do this shit.

KS: Are you glad you did?

WW: No. If I could take it back, I wouldn't do it.

KS: Why?

WW: I'd go to college, man. College is where it's at. I'm glad I'm here defending my country, though. I'm not here for the Iraqi people. I'm here for the American people.

---

* Wold's mother had to give her permission to allow him to join while he was still in high school. He was selected out of boot camp for a special Marine presidential protection unit. He guarded President George W. Bush during his retreats to Camp David.

KS: Do a lot of guys feel the same way that you do?

WW: What's that?

KS: Do you think that a lot of guys feel the same way that you do?

WW: I know that a lot of guys hate these fuckin' shitheads. I'm tired of seein' my brothers get hurt. I've had four of my best friends get killed since I've been here.

KS: Is it frustrating?

WW: It's extremely frustrating. Let me find that guy. They shoot us and run. They hit us with IEDs [improvised explosive devices]. They're cowards. That's why I don't have a problem shootin' any of them.

KS: Do you feel like this offensive has been worthwhile, that you've been able to do something with it?

WW: What's that?

Note: Wold, like a lot of troops in heavy combat, seems to be experiencing some hearing loss.

KS: Do you feel like this offensive has been worthwhile?

WW: I'm gettin' rid of terrorists, I know that. If I can save one American from getting hurt, then I'm doing my job. I don't care about my life. I care about my family's lives. That's the only reason I'm here. I'd come back here in an instant. I hate being here every day, but it's for my family.

KS: Why are you gettin' out?

WW: What's that?

KS: Why are you getting out?

WW: I just wanna be normal. I wanna live a normal life.

KS: Do you think you can after this?

WW: I'm sure I'll be all right. I've changed a lot since I joined the Marine Corps, though. Especially being here. You just . . . I'll never take anything for granted ever again.

KS: Does it harden you?

WW: Um, my last command hardened me pretty much. This place will . . . it'll make you pretty hard. It'll give you some thick skin. [*Explosion*] I'm tired of that, too.

KS: Too much bang there?

WW: Too much big booms.

KS: What will you do after this?

WW: I got a scholarship to play football.

KS: Where are you gonna do that?

WW: WSU. Go Cougs! [*He makes a victory sign.*]

KS: What position?

WW: I'm a linebacker. I had a full-ride scholarship out of high school, but I joined the Marine Corps instead.

KS: Why'd you do that?

WW: Um, my pops always told me it's my duty to serve my country as a young American, so . . . He was killed when I was twelve, so I figured I'd do what he told me to do.

KS: Was he a Marine, too?

WW: Nah, he was in the Army.

KS: How was he killed?

WW: He was murdered when I was twelve.

KS: How did that happen?

WW: I don't know. They never found the guy that did it.*

KS: So you did it in his memory?

WW: What's that?

KS: You joined in his memory?

WW: I just joined to help Americans. I love my family and my fiancée. I never want her to ever have to worry about anybody coming into our country. I'd rather kill 'em in their backyard than have 'em come into our backyard. [*Explosion*] Look at that. [*He points to the orange flameout of a nearby air strike.*] The more I kill here the less I've got to worry about coming into my country.

KS: Does it scare you at all, though? That, like, you have to break into a house like that and you guys have guns pointed at you?

WW: I don't have time to think about that shit. When I first got here, I was always worried about . . . my friend told me today, "Man, you were so worried about getting killed when you first got here." But now, I don't have time to think about that shit. You bust into a house . . . Just like today, I had people pointing AKs at me. And I was thinkin', "I have to shoot them." I shot six people in less than ten seconds. It's just what you've got to do. That shit goes right out the window. And you don't have to push.

---

* The police report says it may have been an accident. Wold's father, Thomas Nelson, was found on an icy road with a broken neck when William was only eleven. Wold's family says he was unsettled by the death and believed it had been a homicide.

[. . .]

KS: If you weren't gonna be deployed, would you stay in the Marine Corps?

WW: Yeah. I don't know if I could do another tour over here. 'Cause the more time you spend here, the more people you wanna kill. Right now, it's . . . I'm so sick of 'em tearin' up my buddies, I just wanna kill 'em all. The more time you spend here, the more time you just wanna get in there and kill 'em.

KS: You think when you get home you'll be able to turn it off?

WW: I hope so. [*His face shows uncertainty.*] I really do. My fiancée's really worried that I'm not gonna come back the same. I'll never tell her what things I did here. I'll never tell anybody. 'Cause I'm not proud of killing people. I'm just proud to serve my country. I never understood it until I got here, you know? I never understood any of it, like, you know, "Hey, I'm defending my country. I'm in the Marine Corps." You don't defend your country until you do something like this. Then you really understand it. The pride aspect really comes out of it. I hate being here but I love it at the same time. It's got its ups and downs. I haven't talked to my fiancée in almost a month. I'm just hoping she's doing good.

KS: Wanna use my phone?

WW: Oh, no, I can't . . . I can't do that.

KS: You're welcome to.

WW: Nah, I couldn't do that.

KS: I asked . . . I let the guys use them all the time, so . . .

WW: Maybe if I see you around.

KS: Yep.

WW: I—

KS: But I let a lot of the guys use them, so it's not a big deal.

WW: I miss everything out here. Our anniversary. My birthday, her birthday. It's the last ones, though, man. Six months, I'll be done. Two months left here.

KS: What do you have to do when you go back to the States? You have to spend three months . . . ?

WW: I'll be, like, three months left in the Marine Corps? Four months?

KS: Just process you out?

WW: I'll get detached out. I'll just work at the gym. I'm, like, a real gym buff. I lost thirty-five pounds since I've been here, so when I get back I really gotta hit the gym real hard.

KS: You gonna go back and play football?

WW: Yeah. I gotta get . . . I weighed two twenty-eight when I got out here, I'm down to about one ninety now. 'Cause I haven't gotten to touch a gym once.

KS: That's hard . . .

WW: It's really hard.

KS: Do you think that some of that anger you have out here, though, is that gonna go back with you, too?

WW: You just learn how to channel your anger. I think I'll be all right. I'm so excited to be a civilian that I'm sure it'll all go away. Like, me and the guy that just got hit, all day today, all we could think today was about goin' home and gettin' a Big Mac and spending the night with our fuckin' . . . our fiancées, you know? It's all we wanna do, just be normal people. This is his third deployment, you know? I can't stand it.

KS: It's hard to do this?

WW: It's not hard to kill people. It's hard not to get killed. My company's got so many casualties it's not even funny.

KS: Yeah, especially in this event. A lot of casualties . . .

WW: [*Yelling*] Hey, we're pushing!

[. . .]

WW: [*Yelling and directing his fireteam*] Hey, Dar, when you come up here, we've got friendlies down here. Hey, we've got friendlies down here! Hold up. Hold up! Hey, listen up! We've got friendlies down to the south! You hear me? Keep your eye on the rooftops and get low!

KS: Which city in Washington?

WW: Vancouver.

KS: It's a nice place.

WW: It's, ah, it's so beautiful. I can't wait to go home. I wanna get . . . um, my motorcycle only got three hundred and fifty miles on it. I can't wait to get back and . . .

KS: What kind of bike you got?

WW: Just bought that new, uh, 636 Ninja. It's Kawasaki.

KS: What's wrong with you, man? You guys always buy those when you go home.

WW: Nah, I bought this, uh . . . I bought it before I came out here. I always wanted a bike.

KS: Is "Willy" short for "William," or is that what you go by?

WW: Uh, William. I go by Willy, though.

KS: You got brothers and sisters?

WW: Uh, three brothers, two sisters.

KS: Older or younger?

WW: I'm the second youngest.

KS: So what do they think about you being out here?

WW: They can't stand it. My little sister . . . if you ever see this, I love you, 'cause she writes me all the time. Her and my mom are writing me all the time, the only ones. And my fiancée, and that's the only . . . that's the sole purpose of why I can make it out here. Is family.

KS: Well if I put you on TV, you ought to call them, so they can at least watch it.

WW: What's that?

KS: I said if I put you on TV, you ought to at least call them so they can watch it.

WW: I tried. It's . . . I know I'm gonna be here for the rest of my tour, so . . . it'll be at least a couple more weeks before I get to talk to 'em. Maybe I can get somebody to send 'em an e-mail or something.

KS: Yeah, give me your e-mail address. I mean, 'cause I might use some of this tonight. Feed it out. We feed our stories every night.

WW: I was on TV a few times. I was on CNN twice when the president had, um, chiefs of staff and he had, um, peacekeeping missions up at Camp David.

KS: You did, uh, protection?

WW: When he gets off the helo . . . when the head of state gets off the helo. Then we provide security for him.

KS: So how'd you get to be a sergeant so fast?

WW: I'm only corporal right now, but I'll be a sergeant soon. I'm a good . . . I've always been a good PTer. I got . . . before

I came out here, I'd go the gym every day. You know? I'm a good shot, as you can see today.

KS: How many did you get? Six today?

WW: I shot six out of nine. I could have shot more, but I'm so worried about putting one of my Marines' lives in danger.

KS: How long did that whole sequence take place?

WW: The killing of those nine people?

KS: Yeah.

WW: Maybe thirty seconds. Just because I've got a slow Marine. He froze up on me. He almost got us killed. I can't be mad at him. I get mad at the kid every day because he's a really slow Marine, but I can't get mad at him for that because morally . . . He told me morally he didn't think he should kill him because he didn't realize what was going on at first. Once I told him what to do, he did it. And he's glad that . . . He'll never question my authority ever again. I guarantee it.

KS: They had the weapons pointed at you?

WW: Yeah, I saved his life today. I'm really glad I did, too. I love the kid to death as a man, but as a Marine, he's just not a very good Marine. [*Yelling*] Yeah? No, I don't! What do you need?

[. . .]

WW: [*Sound of tank round hitting a house*] That's how we clear it. That's probably our main objective. That's how we clear a house. That's how the Marines do it. Okay. We don't mess around.

[. . .]

WW: You gotta be careful, man. You ain't got a gun?

KS: Nah. Yeah, we're noncombatants, so we're not supposed to carry 'em.

WW: I couldn't do that. If I'm gonna be somewhere like this, I gotta have me a gun. That's the bad thing about this country. Everybody got a gun.

KS: That's right. Same with Afghanistan. Crazy.

WW: In Afghanistan it's a totally different war. Of course, we're doing sassel ops around here. You know, except for this. This is a . . .

KS: When you say "sassel ops" what does that mean?

WW: In a nutshell, it's when you go around and you're pretty much there for the people, you know? We hand out soccer balls and try to dodge IEDs every day. Make sure everybody's doing good. Keep the schools running. Try to get the Iraqi police up, you know?

KS: Right.

WW: Here, it's not what we're doin'. Too many terrorists here. They eventually want us to do it here but it's never gonna happen. This place is way too bad. Once they start letting the civilians back in, they have to let all the terrorists come back in.

KS: Yep.

WW: There's a lot of terrorists left. They're cowards. They shoot, throw down their weapons and run. If they come out and fight, the Marines will stick it to 'em. Yeah, we take some casualties, but we stick it to 'em. Ain't no mistake the Marines are here. They can't touch us. We get a casualty here and there. I shot six guys today. My Marine shot three others. One room. They can't touch us. That Marine that got shot today? You should have heard what he said in the Humvee. "Wold, you better kill 'em all." I think he said, "Wold, I love you. You better kill 'em all." I don't have no problem doing that. If they're bad, they're dead.

KS: Is he a good friend of yours?

WW: Yeah, he's my one of my best friends. I met him when I first got to the fleet. We've been good friends ever since.

KS: How bad was he hurt?

WW: He took a few rounds. Took one in the arm, one in the shoulder. The sappy plate stopped about five. It was point-blank. He'll be all right. He's a strong guy. He's the only guy I know who'd put a fight up with me. He's a strong guy. He got . . . he's the same situation as me. He's got four months left. He's got a fiancée back home. She's even got the same name as mine. [*Yelling*] Right here!

Note: Wold pushes out into the darkness with his team.

ONLY LATER, AFTER WATCHING the video of Wold many times, did I realize that the interview had revealed nearly all of what Lieutenant Colonel Dave Grossman, in his book *On Killing*, labeled the six stages of response to killing in combat: concern about killing, the actual kill, exhilaration, remorse, rationalization and acceptance.

He writes, "Like Elisabeth Kubler-Ross's famous stages in response to death and dying, these stages are generally sequential but not necessarily universal. Thus some individuals may skip certain stages, or blend them, or pass through them so fleetingly that they do not even acknowledge their presence."

WILLIAM WOLD SEEMED FINE initially when he came home from Iraq, according to his mother, Sandi Wold, when I speak to her by telephone seven years after my conversation with her son in Fallujah. Wold had begged his mother to sign a parental approval form when he wanted to join the Marines at seventeen, taking extra online classes to graduate a year early in order to do so. But after four years of service, he'd had enough.

"They were going to promote him to sergeant, but he didn't want to reenlist. He just wanted to be normal," she says, echoing his own words from our videotaped interview. His much-anticipated separation from the Marine Corps would come in March 2005, but in the interim, she had promised to treat him and a couple of other Marine buddies to a trip to Las Vegas as a coming-home present. She and her second husband, John Wold (William's stepfather, whose last name he took), met the three Marines at the MGM Grand Hotel and got them adjoining rooms next to their own. Sandi was elated to see her son home safe and in one piece and she wanted to see him leave the war in Iraq behind as quickly as possible.

"There's no way I can show you how much I appreciate your willingness to die for me," she remembers telling the three. But she tried her best anyway, going so far as to hire in-room strippers for them through an ad in the Yellow Pages.

"They talked me into buying them suits and renting a

stretch limo. These guys show up and they go out partying that night, these guys are pimped out, I'm spending so much money it's stupid," she says, laughing at the memory. "Those Marines swam down some drinks, just the three of them. The hotel called my room, 'Do these Marines belong to you?' as they're stumbling down the hallways."

When the strippers showed up to the Marines' room, Sandi says, the sound of partying was like its own war zone. Then around midnight there was a loud banging on the adjoining door.

"The door swings open and it's Silly Billy, drunk and laughing, and he introduces us to them [the strippers] . . . I could've gone a lifetime without meeting them," Sandi says.

"He says, 'Mom, I'm going to need an extra twelve hundred dollars.' 'Dude,' she remembers telling him, 'you gotta be fucking shitting me.' But I'm counting the money out, he's dancing around, happy as can be."

The whole trip, she says, was indicative of the closeness of their relationship. He would always stay in touch with his mom even while he was in Iraq.

"He would hang out with the snipers at night," Sandi says, "because they always had sat phones and he would make sure to try and call me almost every week. It would just be, 'Hey, I'm fine, can't talk long, love you. Bye.'

"He was through and through a mama's boy. There wasn't anything he wouldn't share with me," she says. "Sometimes I had to tell him I just don't want to know."

But Sandi says she began to sense something was wrong

after William made a trip back east to see a woman he had met while doing presidential protection duty at Camp David. He had called her his fiancée and said he planned to marry her, but the relationship ended after his visit with her.

"He flies back there and doesn't last twenty-four hours," Sandi says. "He lost it. He calls me and tells me to find him a flight home. 'I can't close my eyes, I can't sleep,' he tells me, 'what's wrong with me?' I think he knew he was so unstable he was going to end up hurting her."

The extent of his post-traumatic stress became clear to Sandi that summer after his discharge.

"Fourth of July was just horrible for him," says Sandi. "Some neighbors had firecrackers they were setting off in the distance."

But for William that set off a circuit that couldn't be grounded.

"He just starts twitching. 'It's going to be okay,' I told him, but he pushed me back and screamed, 'You don't know what's going on in my brain, there's no switch you can shut off what's going on in here!' He's sweating and pacing, just the look in his eyes. It went on for thirty to forty-five minutes. I visibly see his pulse, two fifty to two sixty, he's going to stroke out. How do I stop it? I need to get three octaves above him. That's what Marines respond to. He's looking for someone in authority to take control. Now we're talking insanely loud, I'm screaming at him, 'You need to bring it down!' trying to use military phrases. I start screaming at him, 'Marine, stand down! Marine, stand down! Marine, stand down!' About the fifth time I did it, it had an effect.'"

Wold stopped shouting and began to calm down, perhaps

beginning to realize how much of the war had actually come home with him.

"Afterward I think he was mortified that he was in a position to hurt me," she says. "Before he left for Iraq he had a sparkle in his eye, he cared about people. He made a commitment to his country and he took it seriously. But when he came home, he was torn and tattered. I hired psychologists, everything we tried to do for him.

"On the backside of my house we have a gazebo and there's a pond. It's where I'm talking to you right now," Sandi tells me. "It's the place where you get right with the world. It's surrounded by trees. No one can see you. He loved being here. He loved being here! He lived with us for a while, then bought a house, but after a while said he couldn't live alone anymore. He just couldn't do it."

With everything he had seen and done in Fallujah in November 2004, Wold told medical professionals, he was having difficulty adjusting to civilian life and was struggling with nightmares, flashbacks and emotional numbing. He was diagnosed with severe post-traumatic stress disorder. He had also reportedly suffered from a blast injury in Iraq, which I could find few details about, but medical records indicate he was experiencing serious cognitive difficulties consistent with traumatic brain injury.* Like so many other service members com-

---

* The Mayo Clinic says traumatic brain injury "usually results from a violent blow or jolt to the head that causes the brain to collide with the inside of the

ing back from the wars in Iraq and Afghanistan physically or psychologically damaged, or both, Wold's life began to revolve around a potent cocktail of painkillers, muscle relaxants and antidepressants he used to cope with his injuries.

According to Wold's military and medical records, at some point after his return from Iraq he began abusing the powerful painkiller OxyContin and became addicted to it. Wold grew more restless and agitated, Sandi says, until the day he told her he was going to reenlist. He had been home for a year and a couple of months, much of it spent shuttling between doctors, psychologists and psychiatrists. But few were able to bring him comfort or relief. His frustration fed on what seemed perfect logic in his damaged brain: while his time with the Marines was the source of injuries, it was also the place he felt most protected.

"My brothers will take care of me," he told Sandi.

"We tried to talk him out of it for hours. 'Look what the Marines have done to you already,'" she says. She was desperate to keep him from returning to the place she felt had hurt him the most. "Get an education, be what you want to be. Look at where you're at," she pleaded.

---

skull. An object penetrating the skull, such as a bullet or shattered piece of skull, also can cause traumatic brain injury. Mild traumatic brain injury may cause temporary dysfunction of brain cells. More serious traumatic brain injury can result in bruising, torn tissues, bleeding and other physical damage to the brain that can result in long-term complications or death." According to the 2008 RAND Corporation study "Invisible Wounds: Mental Health and Cognitive Care Needs of America's Returning Veterans," as many as 320,000 of the 1.64 million U.S. troops who have served in Iraq may have suffered some form of traumatic brain injury.

But she says it was already too late. "He wasn't there any-more. The sparkle in his eyes was completely gone. He was hollow."

Sandi says things went farther downhill from there. After he reenlisted he was made a sergeant in the First Light Armored Reconnaissance Battalion, but according to her, he didn't want to return to combat, but rather wanted to work as an armorer doing repair of light weaponry. His unit's respect for his war service evaporated with their realization that he was addicted to OxyContin.

She claims it culminated one night when he told her that three fellow Marines jumped him while he was in his bunk in the barracks and beat him to the point that he developed a stutter.

"He was having a nightmare and they got tired of it," is how Sandi explains it.

Wold's addiction to OxyContin became so obvious the Marines placed him in the Substance Abuse and Rehabilitation Program (SARP) for intensive inpatient therapy. When he failed to successfully complete the program, he was put in the medi-cal hold unit of the Naval Medical Center pending a medical discharge. In only a few short years he had gone from a fearless warrior baptized in some of the fiercest combat in recent military history to a brain-damaged drug addict about to be tossed from the ranks of those to whom he had once brought so much honor.

On November 9, 2006, Wold and two of his friends, Joshua Frey and Nathaniel Leoncio, spent the day together, which culminated in a trip to a tattoo parlor. To his seven other tat-

toos, Wold added one more. On the inside of his right forearm
he got a multicolored design depicting a woman, an eagle and
a banner reading "All American Bad Ass."

They returned to his room around six thirty that night
and planned to watch a movie. According to legal and medical
reports, one of the friends watched Wold try to take his medications again and reminded him he had already done so earlier.
By some accounts, Wold would do this quite often, repeating
doses of medications he had forgotten he'd already taken. Wold
reclined on his bed and put a pinch of dip between his gums as
had become his habit before going to bed when he was deployed
in Iraq. At a certain point in the evening he told his friends he
was not feeling well and was starting to get cold. The friends left
around eleven thirty P.M. with promises to return in the morning for a camping trip they had planned for the weekend.

When Frey and Leoncio came back nine hours later and
knocked on his door, there was no response. They contacted
the front desk at the medical facility and got security to let
them in. They said they found Wold in the same position they
had left him in the night before, lying on his back in his bed,
his dip cup on his chest. But now he wasn't breathing. Frey and
Leoncio began CPR until paramedics arrived and transported
Wold to the emergency room of the Balboa Naval Medical
Center. He was already cold to the touch. They noticed a pink,
frothy sputum in his mouth.

Despite interventions by the medical staff, they couldn't
get him breathing or his heart beating again. An hour later, at
nine thirty-five A.M., he was pronounced dead. William Chris-

topher Wold was twenty-three years old. The day was Friday, November 10, 2006, just two days before the two-year anniversary of the day he had shot the six Iraqi men in the mosque and then spoken to me outside on the streets of Fallujah.

While I had always remembered my interview with him on that day, I didn't find out what happened to him until a year after his death. I had been working with my friend Jeffrey Porter on a documentary about the war in Iraq when he mentioned the footage of Wold he had been screening. We planned to use it in the film but wanted to follow up with him first. Porter made some inquiries with some of the guys from the unit and was told that Wold had committed suicide. We were both stunned. As I knew him, during our short time together, Wold seemed the very opposite of death, fully alive and animated, conflicted but honest. He was the killer that he was trained to be, but an almost impossibly vulnerable one. As I knew him, Wold did not seem to me like the kind of guy who would voluntarily take his own life. He had a clearly defined sense of purpose and duty and was too connected to his family. We shelved the documentary project for lack of time and finishing funds and went on to other things. But when I began writing this book I wanted to revisit the life of William Christopher Wold. I wanted to talk to his family and get more details about what had happened after he returned from Iraq. But first, I got copies of the San Diego County medical examiner's investigative, autopsy and toxicology reports. What I discovered seemed in some ways even sadder and more shocking then the thought of his suicide.

Wold, it seemed, had died from an accidental drug overdose.

According to the reports, agents from the NCIS spoke with Wold's psychiatrist and confirmed that he had been prescribed the following medications: fluoxetine (better known by its brand name Prozac, used to treat depression), quetiapine tablets (brand name Seroquel, an antipsychotic, often used to treat schizophrenia or in conjunction with other drugs to treat depression), clonidine (brand names Catapres, Kapvay, and Nexiclon, a high blood pressure medication), divalproex (brand name Depakote, used to treat mania, depression and epileptic seizures and approved for migraines), and finally clonazepam (brand name Klonopin, a type of drug known as a benzodiazepine, which can decrease abnormal electrical activity in the brain that can lead to seizures or panic attacks).

After his death, when the agents inspected the room they found bottles for the medications Wold had been prescribed, but also something else.

From county medical examiner's investigative report, submitted December 19, 2006:
They also located a small plastic baggie with several pills inside. The baggie was labeled Seroquel but the pills were later properly identified as methadone. Agents counted the medications and spoke with the decedent's psychiatrist. The doctor confirmed the medications that were prescribed included Prozac, Seroquel, Clonidine, Divalproex, and Klonopin. He confirmed that based on the medications remaining in the bottles found in the

room, it appeared the decedent had been using them as prescribed but added that he had not been prescribed methadone and he was probably obtaining them from an outside source. Agents found no signs of a struggle, evidence of foul play, suicide notes, or illicit drugs in the room.

Seven days after Wold's death, an NCIS agent telephoned the medical examiner's office to provide this additional information, which was included in the investigative report.

From county medical examiner's investigative report, submitted December 19, 2006:
During interviews with the decedent's friends, Nathaniel Leoncio and Joshua Frey, they learned that following the tattoos, the decedent reportedly reached into his pocket and offered his friends a pill to help with the soreness. The friends declined and they noted that the decedent took at least one pill before lying down. Before they left the room, they noticed that the pill had "begun to kick in" and they saw him place tobacco into his mouth and lay down. When they returned the following morning the decedent was in the same position he was in when they left his room the previous night.

In his opinion concerning the cause of death, the San Diego County deputy medical examiner wrote the following.

Autopsy Report, November 11, 2006; 0911 Hours

Toxicological studies were positive for methadone (0.32 mg/L), fluoxetine (0.20 mg/L), norfluoxetine (0.33 mg/L), 7-aminoclonazepam (0.07 mg/L), and nordiazepam (trace). The concentration of methadone in his blood is within a range that has been associated with death; and while the other medicines are in low or therapeutic ranges, they can have similar, additive sedating effects, especially in combination with the methadone.

Based on these findings and the history and circumstances of the death as currently known, the cause of death is best listed as "methadone, clonazepam, diazepam, and fluoxetine toxicity" and the manner of death as "accident."

Steven C. Campman, MD, Deputy Medical Examiner

William Christopher Wold, in the opinion of the deputy medical examiner, had been supplementing his prescription medication drug regimen with methadone, a drug best known for treating heroin and other opiate addicts by preventing withdrawal symptoms, reducing the cravings, but not providing the euphoric rush associated with heroin use. But the U.S. Department of Justice's National Drug Intelligence Center says abuse of methadone is on the upswing, especially by heroin and Oxy-Contin users, because of methadone's increasing availability. Because of its effects on the body, which can include slowed breathing and irregular heartbeat, methadone overdoses can be extremely dangerous, leading to "respiratory depression, decreases in heart rate and blood pressure, coma and death."

In Wold's case, as the deputy medical examiner wrote, his prescription drugs were at a therapeutic level in his body but may have provided an additional sedative effect on him, possibly, as his friend noted, resulting in a forgetfulness of at least what prescription medications he had already taken and presumably leading to a similar lack of awareness about the number of doses of methadone he was taking from his plastic baggy.

Regardless, Sandi Wold, like any mother would, says she has many unanswered questions about her son's death. But as a professional private investigator herself, she was willing to push it more than most. She wondered about things, like why she received the insurance money settlement on Wold's death even before she received his body. Was it an effort to keep her from poking around too much? More sinister, though, she claims that after making calls inquiring into his death she received some anonymous telephone threats herself, but when prompted refused to disclose their nature or reveal any other details.

When I found her initially, it was through an image search for Wold on the Internet. His picture was on a car-racing site that Sandi and her husband John hosted. She got into auto racing as a hobby after a life-changing medical diagnosis.

"Back in 1991, I was diagnosed with MS [multiple sclerosis]," Sandi tells me over the telephone. "I woke up one morning with everything on the left side of my body completely paralyzed. I had red flags like double vision and numbness in my legs, which I had ignored. They did an MRI and diagnosed me with MS. The neurologist said, 'You're not going to walk again.'"

That was all the challenge she needed. She pushed herself to overcome the initial onset of the disease symptoms and not only started walking again but decided she wanted to start racing cars as well, which she now does, with John.

"Bill [William] loved the fact I was racing," she says, and while he wanted to join her in the hobby after coming back from Iraq, she said it was just impossible for him; he was unable to keep his own life, let alone a race car, on track. Sandi's husband John said they used some of William's life insurance money to invest in Sandi's GT race car.

"I learned a lot from that young man in his short years," she tells me in an e-mail.

But what seems impossible to her is that her son could survive some of the harshest combat since the Vietnam War and yet not survive his own homecoming and transition to civilian life. While he did his duty for the corps, both protecting the president personally and protecting his nation overseas, she feels the corps did not protect him in the end. This is a belief echoed by psychiatrist Jonathan Shay and others who work with returning veterans. "When you put a gun in some kid's hands and send him off to war," he told me during an interview, "you incur an infinite debt to him for what he has done to his soul."

Despite her anger with the Marines, Sandi Wold knew her son loved the camaraderie of the corps, but she also understood the internal conflict it had caused him. Still, she had him buried in his dress blues, knowing that underneath them, on the right side of his chest, her son bore another tattoo, this one of praying hands with a banner reading, "Only God Can Judge."

Staff Sergeant Mikeal Auton, U.S. Army
1st Battalion, 4th Infantry
The War in Iraq (2004 and 2006)

CHAPTER 2

PULLING THE TRIGGER

*When I got here I found out that pulling the trigger wasn't
as hard as I thought it would be. All except the first one.*

MIKEAL AUTON was a twenty-one-year-old Army specialist who had already killed twelve men in combat when I
first met him in Iraq in the spring of 2004. He was camped with
his unit, an element of the 1st Armored Division, in the searing
heat and the yellow, powdery sands outside the Shiite holy city
of Karbala. It was only May, but members of his 3rd Platoon
extended tarps and camouflage netting from their Bradleys
(armored personnel carriers) and Abrams A1 tanks to create
enough shade to keep from frying in their boots. But circumstances were miserable for these soldiers for reasons far worse
than the heat. After a yearlong tour in Iraq and on the verge
of going home, the 1st Armored Division had been extended
in country for another three months. Twin uprisings of Sunni
insurgents in Fallujah and Shiite militiamen in Karbala and
Najaf triggered a tsunami of instability that threatened to turn

the entire coalition occupation into chaos. Because of their experience and firepower, the 1st Armored was ordered south to take on Shiite cleric Muqtada al-Sadr's Mahdi Army. The fighting had been frequent and bloody, with masses of poorly trained Shiite militiamen flooding the streets with nothing much going for them tactically but their anger. They would fire what American and British troops scathingly referred to as the "Iraqi overhand," an AK-47 held high and purged on full auto and just as likely to slip from their grips and tag their own guys who were unlucky enough to be in front of them when they started shooting. But many more were cut down in battles with the American troops. Some soldiers told me they were disturbed by the sheer numbers of men they could kill during a battle, mowing them down with intersecting fields of fire (troops firing from right and left flanks across a center line), as if they were nothing more than zombies in a B-movie.

During their downtime, the 3rd Platoon's soldiers did what all soldiers do: cleaned their weapons, played cards and bullshitted with each other. I witnessed the taunting and merciless teasing, but also moments of clear-eyed introspection that made the soldiers, once again, seem like the vulnerable and innocent high school seniors they had mostly been just a year or two ago. But then, as I wrote in an online article for MSNBC.com at the time, they also did things like this:

Nearby one soldier passes a couple of American flag patches to another. In between the bars on the patch are the words, handwritten in ink: Dirty for Dirty.

They are calling cards to put on the bodies of dead enemies, a non-sanctioned post-mortem psych-out. Something to let the Muktada al-Sader's militia know who they are and what they are up against. The same soldiers tell me about a recent fight they were in in which a Shiite militiaman popped into an alleyway and began firing his AK-47 at a tank. "You could see the turret swivel around, train its 50 [caliber machine gun] on the guy and fire. It blasted a huge hole right through his middle." He shows dinner plate size circumference with his hands.

Auton, I noticed, had a small chain attached to a belt loop on the front of his BDUs (battle dress uniform), which dangled into one of his pockets. When I asked him to show me what was tethered on the other end he lifted the chain from his pocket and retrieved a tiny book, which he flipped open and thumbed from right to left. Its pages were covered with Arabic script, a miniature Koran. Auton said it had been a gift given to him by his Turkish girlfriend, whom he met while stationed in Germany.

While there was a certain irony to a Christian American soldier carrying a Koran into battle against Muslim enemies, I found it more interesting that Auton simply ignored the grief that other soldiers gave him for having it. He carried himself with the rare confidence of someone who didn't have to sell you anything, least of all his reasons for doing something. While he was like so many other troops who carried some special token into battle, Auton's choice of lucky charm was my first clue that he was not just your average grunt. This was a soldier, I believed, who would answer my most difficult questions, such as the one I asked him next: How did he feel about all the killing he had done?

"When I got here I found out that pulling the trigger wasn't as hard as I thought it would be," Auton said from the back of the Bradley where we sat talking, with the troop hatch open. "All except the first one. It was 'Wow, I just killed a man,'" he said. "You start thinking he coulda been a guy just protecting his family. But then you think, 'Okay, he's running around out here with an AK-47 shooting at us,' then you just get over it. Move on."

Auton did move on but he never forgot the details of his first kill. It was in a Sunni section of Baghdad known as al-Adhamiyah. Auton's platoon was part of a QRF, or Quick Reaction Force, which stands ready to respond when another unit is attacked or needs help.

The platoon was ordered on a mission one night and rolled out of their base with tanks and Bradleys. They didn't have to wait long for enemy contact. Almost as soon as they pushed into the neighborhood they were hit with rocket-propelled grenades and AK-47 fire. Most Bradleys are configured with three crew, a vehicle commander, driver and gunner, and carry six or seven additional troops crammed in a small hold in the rear. While the hammer of automatic rifle fire against the metal can make the troops feel like they're inside a steel drum that's being pounded on both sides, a rocket-propelled grenade round is much worse. It can be roughly equivalent to the explosive depth charges used against a submarine, whose concussion can send shock waves that leave both ears and bodies ringing.

After maneuvering to a position where the Bradley's hatch could be lowered and the soldiers dismounted, Auton and members of his fireteam set up fighting positions using buildings and alleyways for cover. Once the shooting started, Auton says, the more restrictive rules of engagement went out the window; anything on the street was considered a fair target.

"I was set up on a corner with my squad leader and we had a guy headed in our direction who had his hands in his pockets," says Auton.

While they couldn't tell if he was carrying a weapon or not, the squad leader gave Auton the order to shoot him. Auton peered through the optical scope on his M4 rifle, lined up the reticle crosshairs on the man's head, then gently squeezed the trigger. The bullet dropped slightly over the hundreds of feet of distance, but so did Auton's target.

"I shot him in the throat at about two hundred to two hundred and forty meters. He fell to his knees, gasping for air."

Auton and the squad leader moved in closer to inspect. The guy was still alive but hunched over. But Auton said they still weren't sure what he had in his pockets.

"What do you want me to do?" Auton asked his squad leader. The squad leader hesitated for a few seconds.

The choice to complete the unfinished process of taking a life in war leads directly to consequences unknown. Some would say it carries twice the moral weight by offering the soldier another chance to reconsider the delivery of a mortal blow. But which decision will be easier for the soldier to live with, confirmation of the original intent to kill, or watching an enemy suffer by allowing him to continue to live or die without intervention?

This is perhaps the most poignant dilemma in Erich Maria Remarque's classic novel of World War I *All Quiet on the Western Front*, in which German soldier Paul stabs a French soldier who has stumbled into his trench, but instead of dying immediately the man's agony is both intimate and prolonged. Paul nearly goes mad watching him suffer from just a few feet away: "These hours . . . The gurgling starts again—but how slowly a man dies! For this I know—he cannot be saved. Indeed, I have tried to tell myself that he will be, but at noon this pretence breaks down and melts before his groans. If only I had not lost my revolver crawling about, I would shoot him. Stab him I cannot."

Here, on this street in Iraq, for Auton and his squad leader, the questions had real consequences. Had the man been sub-dued? Was he no longer a threat or did he still conceal some unseen harm? The choice they would make would have a life-time impact on them and would have to be justified on legal as well as personal and moral grounds.

The squad leader, believing the Iraqi could still be a threat, said, "Finish it." Auton raised his rifle to the man a second time.

"I fired two rounds in his ear at two feet away." His brains splattered across the street and blood seeped out in a large, dark crimson pool. When they pulled the now-dead man's hands from underneath him and checked his pockets, Auton said they found a little black fragmentation grenade with the pin still in place. Auton said he and his squad set up on another corner and repeated the procedure several more times that night. When someone would run through the streets, his squad leader would spot him with the narrow beam of his SureFire flashlight and Auton would take the shot.

"I wasn't there to care," Auton said without any affection of false bravado. To him, it was a matter of ultimate practicality. "You don't hold on to it. There's a time for remorse, there's a time to think about what happened. But it wasn't that moment. You have to just be thankful it wasn't you."

I track Auton down by e-mail six years later. He's still with the same unit based in Germany, but now leading a platoon as a staff sergeant rather than a member of a squad. He has done well by the Army and he feels they've done the same by him. And despite another deployment to Iraq, two years after we first met in Karbala, his attitude has changed little. He plans on being a "lifer," making the Army his career. He broke up with his Turkish girlfriend after his deployment ended but tells me in an e-mail from Germany that he still carries his lucky charm.

"I do still have the small Koran and will keep it until the day I die. My last deployment I had the Koran with me as well, even though her and I had been split up for over two years. I will carry it again when I go to Afghanistan in the near future."

Auton's perspective on killing hasn't changed much either, despite the fact that he's now an older, experienced leader. "I must say that with my time deployed I feel outstanding for every life that I have taken," he says in an e-mail. "I know now that those men that I personally killed would have killed me or my buddy to the left or right at any chance they could have gotten. I am glad I am the one who could take their life. I feel as if I saved many lives by doing so. I would do it all a million times over if I had to or need to for my fellow Soldiers and country!!"

While this response might seem overly gung-ho or even callous for those who haven't shared his experiences, during my time with him Mikeal Auton convinced me that he's a reasonable, polite and well-adjusted individual. But unlike many of his fellow soldiers struggling with their experiences of killing and seeing others killed, he, at least at for now, seems unfazed by the deadly business in which he has been employed for the last third of his life.

Psychiatrists, psychologists, sociologists, anthropologists and all other manner of social scientists have struggled with the idea of killing and how we live with ourselves in the aftermath of having taken the lives of others. The psychological concept of the "shadow self" looms large here. The idea was first advanced by Swiss psychiatrist Carl Jung, who wrote in his study *Psychology and Religion: West and East*, "Everyone carries a shadow and the less it is embodied in the individual's conscious life, the blacker and denser it is."

It's a Western variation on the Chinese philosophy of yin and yang, where opposite forces, light and dark, masculine and feminine, coexist and are interdependent on each other. But unlike yin and yang, where these opposites are not necessarily distinctions between good and evil, Jung believed the shadow was a receptacle for human darkness, but also a place of creativity. Many scholars of war have interpreted the shadow as the best way to explain the human capacity for killing and our response to it.

In *The Warriors: Reflections on Men in Battle*, the philosopher and World War II combat veteran J. Glenn Gray wrote, "Becoming a soldier was like escaping from one's own shadow. To commit deeds of violence without the usual consequences that society visits upon the violent seemed at first a bit unnatural but for many not unpleasant. All too quickly it could become a habit."

For a rare few, the shadow is the dominant or conscious, rather than subconscious, force in life. They're commonly referred to as sociopaths or psychopaths. According to Dr. Martha Stout in her book *The Sociopath Next Door*, the 4 percent of the American population in this category lacks any trait of empathy or remorse even when it comes to killing other people. Though there are no clear statistics on the number of sociopaths in the military as opposed to the rest of society (there are psychological screenings in place intended to weed them out from military service), it would seem a fair number would tend to gravitate toward a profession where lack of emotion in the face of death could be considered a virtue.

For the other 96 percent of us, our ability to kill may simply be enabled by our shadow self, but its consequences are borne by our other half. For some, that burden is permanently debilitating, regardless of the circumstances. For others, it may be compartmentalized or shuffled somewhere in the folds of the mind, where it's contained and does not interfere daily with an otherwise normal life. And it may be this group in which the early experiences of one's life profoundly affect that person's ability to reabsorb their shadow self into its interstitial space and keep it fully in check when not at war.

AUTON, I REALIZE, LIVES in that place where bullets and background intersect. The hard realities of rural poverty he experienced as a child and that he learned to contain, rather than let them define him, prepared him quite thoroughly, it seems, for the things he would have to do in war.

"To be honest with you—this sounds weird or hard to understand—you just put it behind you," Auton tells me during a telephone call. "You can't live in the past; you have to live in the present."

Far from judging him, I have great respect for his reasoning and his ability to steady himself in the face of powerfully destabilizing experiences. I envy the inner strength and resolve by which he has "soldiered" on, while I, who have taken a life by the confused incompetence of inaction rather than pulling a trigger, sometimes have had difficulty in finding both meaning and worth for my own life in the aftermath of the incident.

And for Auton, living in the present is certainly preferable, considering how he grew up in rural Lenoir, North Carolina, bordering the Pisgah National Forest, sixty miles northwest of

Charlotte. Auton was the third youngest of four siblings, an older brother and sister and a younger brother.

"I grew up in a very poor family. I remember days where I would heat water on a kerosene heater in order to have hot water for a bath," says Auton. "I always knew what I would have for dinner when I got home from school because it was always cabbage and potatoes."

Auton's parents were divorced and he says his mother focused more on other men than her children.

"My sister and I were always close to each other and she is still the only one I speak to this day out of my family. My sister and I came home from school one day and found a note on the kitchen table with some money, I think around three hundred dollars. I was around ten years old if I remember right. The note said, 'Here is the next two months' rent, I hope you can find a place to live.'" He says his mother left with a man she had known for a few weeks.

His sister, Elizabeth, was fifteen at the time and had an older boyfriend whose family took them both in and raised them, Auton says, like they "were their own children," for the next eight years of his life.

But by his senior year in high school he became rebellious and moved in with some other friends, hitting the streets at night, drinking and getting into a little bit of trouble. He says he struggled through his senior year of high school but kept it together just enough to graduate. His sister married the same man she was with when their mother left them. But Auton says he has no idea where his mother or brothers are. He broke off relations with his father when he refused to take them in after they were abandoned. He says because he was abandoned by his parents a lot of people looked at him as a lowlife, a "bottom-feeder." That motivated him to prove them wrong and do something with his life. That's when he decided to join the Army.

To Auton, the Army became the family he felt he never had. It seemed to give him all the basic things his own did not: food, shelter, clothing, money and, perhaps equally important, people to share the challenges and successes of life with. But while the Army helped him to feel like he was part of a community, Auton's past taught him not to invest too deeply in emotions. Being able to contain the hardships and unhappiness of his childhood allowed him to "move on," as he said, and live in the present. He would use the same skills, successfully, to push past the darkness and trauma of war.

It wasn't always easy. When Auton became a leader in the Army, he became responsible for the health and well-being of his men, which required a closeness that made him more vulnerable, though as always he did his best to contain that as well. When Auton was deployed again to Iraq in 2006, his unit was focused on helping to clear insurgents out of Ramadi in the Sunni-dominated al-Anbar Province. A well-liked twenty-two-year-old sergeant named Edward Schaeffer was part of Auton's squad. Auton says Schaeffer was so smart, they nicknamed him "the Brain." But that November, while on patrol, the lead vehicle of Auton's convoy hit an improvised explosive device and the Bradley burst into flames. The driver was Schaeffer. He was blown out of the hatch and landed ten feet away in a ball of flames. Another soldier put him out with a fire extinguisher. His burns were so severe, he later died from them. Auton admits the death affected him.

"I don't think I was sad. I was angry more than anything," Auton says. "He was such a young guy. It motivates you to be there even more and to find them [the attacker]. I don't know if we got the exact one, but we got plenty of them. We cordoned off the area, did raids for the next three hours—it wasn't knocking, it was hard raids."

While Auton can be stirred by the loss of one of his men, his mostly unemotional nature sometimes gives him the leverage to understand things his more emotionally charged comrades can't. When Auton does his job, killing the enemy, he doesn't feel the need to hate or dehumanize them. If they're a threat to him and his men they're dead. But since he doesn't choose to see them as anything less than himself, as anything other than warriors doing their jobs, he can also offer them the same respect when they prove particularly worthy and tenacious adversaries, as did one he encountered during that same tour, in a city on the western border of Iraq.

After searching a barn in a nearby village and finding explosives and suicide vests buried in the hay, Auton moved his fireteam to the house next door to continue the search. They cleared the house floor by floor, from bottom to top. But when they reached the final floor of the house it appeared to be completely empty. They all relaxed for a moment . . . until they heard the unmistakable sound of metal on concrete. Their eyes opened wide as an olive-green Russian-made grenade came rolling across the floor toward them. "Grenade," one of the soldiers yelled, and they all dove for cover as the small powerful explosion cratered the floor and forced shards of metal into the concrete walls on all sides. They were so surprised by the attack that they felt whoever had tossed the grenade might as well have been invisible.

"We know we cleared the room," says Auton, "so we figured the guy had to actually be inside the wall somewhere." That's when they called in the EOD unit, Explosive Ordnance Disposal, the same kind of specialists depicted in the Oscar-winning film *The Hurt Locker*. The EOD team planted C4 plastic explosives around the walls and leveled half the building. Once the dust cleared, Auton saw a vent duct above the stairwell. If the attacker had been in the vent, he had to be dead now. But that thought disappeared as soon as his team began taking fire from the vent. They returned fire, pumping more than a thousand rounds into the hole, but according to accounts from the soldiers, the stubborn sniper continued to fire back.

"I personally threw five grenades into the hole and the guy wouldn't go down," Auton says with a laugh. After a few hours of exchanging fire with the sniper, EOD planted C4 in what was left of the remaining walls and turned the entire building into rubble with a huge explosion. When the dust and smoke cleared, they saw the sniper lying in a pile of broken cinder blocks and concrete. But Auton and his men were astounded by what happened next. Like one of the machines out of the Terminator films, the Iraqi seemed almost impossible to kill.

"The dude sat up with his AK-47 from the rubble, turned and looked at us—he had to be on adrenaline or something," says Auton. Another sergeant tossed a grenade at him, finally ending the five-hour standoff.

"You rarely encounter someone like that. This guy gave his position up. He could've hid and we wouldn't have known he was there. You give respect for something like that, for bravery or whatever else. I can clearly picture him, skinny, five foot nine, clean-shaven face, black hair, black T-shirt, pair of jeans, and his whole body full of holes after the grenade."

As Auton prepares for his third deployment, this one to Afghanistan, he's now engaged to a German woman but uncertain if they'll be able to work out their differences. She wants to stay in Germany, which Auton says he also loves, but he will have to go wherever the Army decides to send him. He will not abandon the family that he believes has given him his true place in this world. He already knows this will be his career no matter how many times he gets deployed. Somehow, despite what he's had to do, this work has filled the empty spaces in him and given him both stability and a sense of calm and purpose. He tells me so in an e-mail.

"The army is the simplest job you can have. All you have to do is be where you are supposed to be on time and do what you are told," says Auton. "The higher the rank you get the better the job. I am at the point in my career where now I issue the orders and teach the soldiers, this I love to do! I can retire at 39 yrs old. Where else in the civilian life could I do that? Also, everything is paid for. The only worry I have is the loss of my life or a soldier's life, and I have come to peace with both of these."

POSTSCRIPT

In March 2012, I got an e-mail from Auton telling me that he got married in October 2011 in a small German town called Wetzlar. He told me that he also passed the Army's twenty-four-day Special Forces assessment and selection process at Fort Bragg, North Carolina, less than two hundred miles from where he grew up. In the fall he would attend the five-phase qualification course. If successful, Auton would wear the dagger-and-crossed-arrow flash of one of the most elite, highly trained and legendary units of the American military, the Green Berets.

PART II

The Wounds of War

What's It Like to Be Shot, Bombed or Burned in Combat?

The brightest best thing in my life was the war and there won't be anything better. And the blackest lousiest thing in my life was also the war, and there won't be anything worse. So my life has been lived.

—Arkady Babchenko, Russian soldier, journalist
From *One Soldier's War*, Arkady Babchenko, translated
by Nick Allen (Grove Press, 2008).
Babchenko was a conscript for the first Chechnya
campaign in 1995 and volunteered for the second in 1999.

Lance Corporal James Sperry, U.S.M.C.
3rd Battalion, 1st Marines
The War in Iraq (2004)

CHAPTER 3

||||||||||||||||||||||||||||||||||||||||

SURVIVOR'S GUILT

*I am only twenty-four and
have lived a life I wish on no one.*

REDEMPTION CAN come from the most unlikely places.
Mine is a present from a war-damaged twenty-four-year-
old in Lebanon, Illinois, who e-mailed these words to me.

Dear Mr. Sites
You were imbedded [sic] with 3rd Bn/ 1st Mar. Div.
during operation phantom fury. I was the Marine that
you helped care me to saftey after i was shot by a sniper.
I want to say thank you very much for helping me out.
I was wondering if you had taken any photos of me
during that time of injury and any of my fallen friends.
i have lost twenty friends in this war and would like to
get as many pictures as I can. I will pay what ever you
want for the pictures. Thank you again from the bottom
of my heart for all you did for me. i now have a three

year old child that would nevr of came if was for your
help. I will for ever be in your debit. Thanks
James Sperry
0311/USMC/RET.**

His note arrives at a time when I'm feeling worthless, when I peer into the mirror in the morning at my tired and puffy face and wonder what right I have to be here at all. I'm struggling to write; I'm struggling with alcohol, drinking a fifth of vodka or whiskey every other day; I'm struggling to find some hope and a sense of purpose outside a war zone. For an elusive moment, James Sperry has given me both.

But the credit he offers me is undeserved. Though I did pick up an end of his stretcher, along with five Marines, during Operation Phantom Fury in Fallujah, Iraq, it was hardly an act that saved his life. Military medics and later surgeons were responsible for that. I was simply an extra hand to help move him from an open flatbed truck to an armored troop carrier for evacuation. While I had been embedded with his unit, I had never seen Sperry until the first day of the ground offensive. He was lying on his back in an alleyway. He looked dazed as his head was bandaged by a Navy corpsman. I remember zooming in, as I videotaped him, on the crimson beads of a rosary hanging out of one of the trouser pockets of his BDUs. I wondered if he still believed in their power now that he was

---

* All e-mails and Internet postings displayed as written.

wounded; maybe he believed in them even more. I wouldn't learn until years later that it wasn't even his rosary.

It was strange that Sperry's note had a consoling effect on me, considering that up until that point my actions had remained in my mind over the years not as an act of kindness on my part, but as a sin of omission. For while I helped carry Sperry to safety, and I'm glad I did, a few hours earlier I had also walked away from an older Iraqi man slowly bleeding to death after being shot in the head by a Marine sniper (detailed in the prologue). Sperry's note has not absolved me of what I did not do, but in a small way it affirmed what I did, and for now, that has made some difference to me.

During my Nieman Fellowship at Harvard, Sperry and I begin a series of conversations over Skype. But he's struggling too. Like me, he's using alcohol to self-medicate, but also pot and the dozen prescription medications that are part of his daily postwar routine. He sometimes disappears for weeks at a time without picking up for our calls. I plead with him by e-mail but still silence. Eventually he reemerges, but I know it will take meeting face-to-face if I'm ever going to get his complete story. When he finally resurfaces, I convince him to allow me to visit him over Christmas break on a one-day stopover on my way to see my parents in Arizona. He agrees but then disappears again. Just when I'm about to give up on him, he surfaces and confirms my visit, just five days before I'm scheduled to arrive.

It's already dark at five thirty P.M. when I pull up to James Sperry's house on a small, unlighted cul-de-sac in a small

southern Illinois town about forty-five minutes east of down-
town Saint Louis. It's two days before Christmas and my flights
have been predictably delayed by weather and overbooking
this time of year. I was supposed to arrive nearly five hours
ago. I double-check the address because there are no cars in
the driveway and no lights on in the house. Several of the other
houses on the cul-de-sac are wired for the holidays, plastic San-
tas and candy canes putting off the only illumination on the
street. Sperry's house is bare. I knock on the door and already
begin to feel a little strange and intrusive. Though our paths
crossed six years ago on the embattled streets of Fallujah, we
were strangers then, as well as now.

Sperry and I have been building trust, over the last two
months, trying to peel back the years and details of what happened since we last met. It has been a humbling and trying process beset by the challenges of both his responsibilities, which
include a wife and three-year-old daughter, as well as the physical and psychological wounds that require a chef's salad worth
of drugs every day, including clonazepam for anger (Sperry calls
it his chill pill), citalopram for adrenaline deficiency (overtaxed
during his deployment), hydrocodone for headaches, mirtaza-
pine and Ambien to sleep, prazosin to head off his nightmares
and a self-injecting EpiPen-type device like those carried by
people allergic to bee stings, which Sperry administers in the
case of debilitating migraines that send him quivering into a
dark closet with a blanket over his head until he can fall asleep.
Sperry, admittedly, also heavily self-medicated with alcohol
back at Camp Pendleton for nearly two years after his return

from Iraq, drinking with other Iraqi vets from early morning until he passed out at night, filling the days with death-seeking stunts like gunning his Japanese sport motorcycle (a nearly stereotypical impulse buy for many returning vets) down the freeway at over a hundred miles an hour—drunk.

He said he'd probably be dead already if it hadn't been for the Vietnam-era veterans he met after being committed to a VA psych ward for a month following a failed suicide attempt. They helped convince him that while alcohol could temporarily numb his feelings, its long-term depressant effect would eventually kill him. Sperry said he had since mostly replaced alcohol with marijuana (the exception, supposedly, is a few beers now and then). While it was actually VA doctors who recommended he start using marijuana medicinally, Sperry said, it was unlawful for them to dispense it. Instead he now buys it from a former high school buddy. "It's the only thing that has really helped me," he said.

Sperry said while the pot leveled him out, it was his daughter Hannah that really gave him any reason to live. He explained the challenges he faced daily in an e-mail before my visit.

November 2009 (e-mail from Sperry to me)

I have lost twenty friends and would love to have
any photos available. Transition has been extremely
difficult. I have nightmares almost nightly and migraine
headaches every other day. I don't have any friends
beside my close family because I feel like I can't relate
to anyone. I did try to kill my self three years ago before

the birth of my daughter. I spent a month in a mental institution. I have almost no short-term memory. I can't do school at all I have failed out of every class almost. I use to be smart but since my several traumatic brain injures I can't do much besides housework and raising my daughter. The only way I sleep is by pills. I take pills for everything my extreme anger, depression, anxiety, and panic attacks. I was way to young to experience the death of all my friends. I don't want to get close to any one because I don't want to have anymore hurt in my life. I can't be away from my family for any long period of time with out having extreme panic attacks and anxiety because I am not there standing guard over the people I have left to love. I am not normal I am in a different reality then the majority of easy going Americans. I wake up every morning hurting in my hips, back, shoulders, and head. I wonder how it is going to be when I am thirty years old. I am only twenty-four and have lived a life I wish on no one. The bright and shining star in my life and the reason I get up and go thru the routines is to watch the innocent of my daughter. I look forward to hearing from you. Sincerely, James Sperry

Within a few seconds of my knocking, Sperry arrives at the door wearing a T-shirt and jeans and socks but no shoes. He's accompanied by two dogs, Carly, a newly acquired, rambunctious bull terrier that his daughter, Hannah, named after the popular Nickelodeon program *iCarly*, and a spaniel–Saint Bernard mix named Everett, who, like Sperry, is shuffling along and showing a bit more age than he has.

We shake hands. I tell Sperry he looks better than the last time I saw him, through the viewfinder of my camera. He laughs, but Everett backs away. I reach out a hand, palm down, for him to sniff, but he's wary, moving down the hallway away from me. When I stand upright, he lets out several deep woofs.

"Wow," Sperry says, surprised, "that's really strange. I've never seen him bark at anyone . . . ever."

I'm just as surprised. I've had dogs for a good portion of my life and understand the techniques for lowering their sense of threat level. But perhaps Everett has absorbed some of Sperry's postwar hypervigilance, a common symptom, according to psychologists and psychiatrists, of combat veterans suffering from post-traumatic stress disorder. It is, experts believe, a continuation of the vigilance soldiers had to adopt to survive for prolonged periods in war zones, as well as an effect of their loss of the ability to trust others. Many dog owners learn to trust the instinct of their animals. I hope Sperry doesn't read too much into it. Despite the pleasantries, I can already see the palpable discomfort my arrival has created for him. A phone call is different than a visit; there's separation and the ability to control the conversation by ending it whenever one chooses. However, now I'm here in his living room at my own request, to see and talk to him face-to-face about his life after war. And it's a story, despite his delays, I think he wants to tell.

Sperry's wife, "Cathy" (she asked that her real name not

be used in this book), joins us at the dining room table. They were sweethearts since freshman year of high school and actually joined the Marines together on an early-enlistment package their junior year.

She wanted to be a photojournalist but didn't get the occupation guarantee in writing from the recruiter. She ended up in diesel generator repair instead and worked stateside, never deploying to Iraq or Afghanistan. Sperry wanted infantry, and, of course, got it. I open my computer and play for them the video I shot the day Sperry was wounded. (Watch the video of Lance Corporal James Sperry: https://www.youtube.com/watch?v=L7hzClvEBxU&feature=plcp.) This is the first time he's ever seen it, but strangely, for Cathy, it's the second. She first saw it while doing her post–boot camp military occupational specialty (MOS) training as a diesel mechanic at Marine Corps Base Camp Lejeune in North Carolina. She was walking back to her quarters when my NBC News field report from Fallujah began playing on a large-screen TV at an outside courtyard. Though his face was obscured by blood and bandages, Cathy says she knew it was James immediately. Now, all these years later, they are transfixed by the images, watching as my camera zooms in on the maroon-colored plastic rosary hanging out of Sperry's pants.

When I first shot the video, I had assumed it was Sperry's talisman, a lucky charm like the ones many soldiers carried into battle. But one night as we talked on the telephone I learned there was much more to the story. In fact, it was a touchstone to one of several critical events in Iraq that Sperry acknowledges changed him from an earnest and hopeful teenager into a stone-hearted Marine.

Sperry's best friend in the Marines was a Mexican-American kid named Fernando Hannon, whom he met during basic training at Camp Pendleton. While Hannon didn't plan on making the military a career, he did want to follow in the footsteps of his father, Spurgeon, a Vietnam War veteran. At six foot four, Hannon was a gentle giant, Sperry said, a sweet soul who prayed daily that he would never have to kill anyone during his deployment in Iraq. Hannon's family meant everything to him and when his sister contracted cancer right before their deployment to Iraq, Hannon left Camp Pendleton without permission to see her. Not wanting his friend to get into trouble, Sperry found ways to cover for him until he got back.

While he wanted to make his father proud by his military service, Hannon's real dream was to become a chiropractor and marry his high school sweetheart, a girl named Ruth Ponce. Ponce was apparently so smitten with Hannon that she asked him to their senior prom. Hannon, it seems, was just as taken with her. Sperry said that Hannon's favorite subject was his future wedding with Ponce. To Hannon, a wedding represented the happiest moment in a person's life and he had been saving up for his, even before he met Ruth. Hannon told Sperry he had already amassed $48,000 for the big day, from the odd jobs and part-time work that he had been doing since he was a child.

"He was like a woman," Sperry said, remembering their

talks with a smile. "He would describe in detail the way the hall would be decorated, what kind of colors, even the type of cake. He said he never played army when he was little. He played prince and princess. That's what he dreamed about more than anything."

Unlike Sperry, Hannon was religious, raised Catholic. He prayed frequently and even brought a rosary from home when he deployed to Iraq. Hannon was also adamant about not wanting to kill anyone, so, Sperry said, he did his best to help his friend avoid pulling the trigger. While their company, India, was primarily deployed outside Fallujah in a former schoolhouse in the nearby village of al-Karma, Sperry and Hannon would frequently be ordered to guard traffic control point #8, or what was commonly known as the Cloverleaf, an elevated loop road that provided a passageway both into and out of Fallujah. Late afternoon on August 14, 2004, Sperry and Hannon were both on guard duty at the Cloverleaf. Initially, Hannon was assigned to the more dangerous post, facing into Fallujah, where insurgents were still in control and often sent suicide car bombers to attack the Marine position. Sperry was assigned to the opposite post, facing the road that led to Baghdad. Sperry switched with Hannon that day, as he sometimes had before, taking the inside post knowing it would be more likely to see action. This would spare Hannon from potentially having to take a life. But on this night the violence came from the outside, a suicide car bomber driving from Baghdad toward Fallujah and the very place where Hannon stood guard.

"There was a huge explosion," Sperry said, "and the entire

forward post was gone. I ran over to it after some of the smoke cleared. I saw Hannon on the side of the road. Both arms and legs were broken. He had shrapnel in his chest and one of his eyeballs was gone."

But even with all his wounds, Hannon asked after another Marine, wondering if he was hurt. Geoffrey Perez, a buddy of Hannon and Sperry since boot camp, was killed in the blast. Hannon would die on the medevac flight to Baghdad, though Sperry wouldn't learn of his best friend's death until hours later.

While Hannon was choppered out, Sperry stayed on post at the Cloverleaf through the night. When darkness fell the post came under attack again. Insurgents fired 81 mm mortars all around them. Sperry says the rounds were getting so close that dust was shaking from the building where they were taking cover.

"You never really feel safe, but after a while you feel like you just want to stop running," he recounted with a weary eloquence.

As the shelling continued, and with Perez's death and Hannon's soon-to-be-fatal injuries weighing heavily on him, Sperry began to lose his will to live. He unbuckled the chin strap to his Kevlar helmet and placed it on the ground next to him. Slowly he pulled at the edges of his body armor until the hook-and-loop fasteners gave way. He lay on his back, his vest open, his most fragile organs exposed, waiting, even hoping, for a round to find him through the darkness. It never did.

When he awoke the next day, still alive, Sperry says he was a different person. He became skeptical of the mission and with each passing day there was a growing sense of dread that his own fate was sealed.

"I told my wife, 'I'm not coming home, everyone is going down.' I told her I loved her and that was it. We weren't accomplishing anything. She kept saying, 'Don't say that.' I just had a gut feeling. I mean every time we went out, we got hit. I thought it was just a matter of time before I got killed."

When he got back to the schoolhouse base in al-Karma and learned of Hannon's death, Sperry says the loss began the process that would soon completely strip him of his innocence and force him to acknowledge that the world was a cruel and ruthless place. In this unforgiving reality, Sperry wanted a reminder of the gentle spirit of his friend, who was willing to die in this war but would not kill. He threaded Hannon's maroon rosary through the front belt loop of his combat fatigues with the cross nesting inside his right pocket and never again went outside the wire without it.*

Sperry was almost certain he would die in Iraq. There had been so many close calls already, some of them darkly comic. Early in the deployment, without fully armored Humvees, Sperry had to devise his own homemade turret, in which he placed a sheet of plywood over the soft-topped Humvee and then piled sandbags into a ring in which he sat, "Indian-style,"

---

* "Outside the wire" is an American military term used to denote the defensive perimeter surrounding any type of forward operating base. Inside the wire is considered a protected space, outside the wire unprotected.

along with his M249 SAW (squad automatic weapon) on an improvised mount.

"Whoever was driving would hit the brakes once in a while and they'd laugh while I'd go rolling off the top of the vehicle," says Sperry. With nothing to secure him or the sandbags to the roof of the "Hillbilly Humvee," he was vulnerable and unprotected. One day as they were getting ready to cross a bridge back to their base in al-Karma, everyone in the vehicle flinched at the sound of a loud pop and a puff of smoke next to the vehicle on the side of the road. An Explosive Ordnance Disposal team was called to the site and found three 155 mm artillery rounds daisy-chained together, buried in the palm grove adjoining the road. It was most likely command detonated, meaning someone nearby was watching and tried to explode the roadside bomb as the American forces drove past. The blasting cap fired, making the popping sound, but the artillery shells did not. If they had, everyone agreed that given his precarious position on top, Sperry would've likely been launched from the roof like it was a medieval catapult.

"If it would've gone off we would've been toast," he says. "We laughed about it later, called it the world's smallest IED."

On another occasion Sperry and squad mates went to provide security for an EOD team investigating a taxi that insurgents had rigged with a multiple rocket launcher in the trunk. When the device malfunctioned it sent a shower of rockets into the town, one of which impaled a man who just happened to be sitting in his car at the wrong place and the wrong time. As the EOD team moved up to the taxi in the aftermath, it also exploded, launching the two bomb technicians forty feet in the air, killing them.

But sometimes, Sperry says, it was the much less dramatic but seemingly personal moments of violence that would make him come momentarily unhinged. One evening, at the base in al-Karma, Sperry was on lookout duty, perched on the school-house roof, sweeping the green fields in front of him for signs of movement, while the horizon turned the color of burning cigarette ash. There was a flash in the distance and Sperry dropped instinctively to his knees as a tracer round streaked over his head. At that moment for him, it was one bullet too close and one too many.

"I freaked out, after," Sperry says. "I fell to the ground with tears in my eyes. It might've been the adrenaline rush, I just don't know. Corporal Krueger came up to the roof after seeing what had happened and said to me, 'You're the luckiest motherfucker ever.'"

There would be other roadside bombs and nightly mortars, patrol missions and house searches. In another attack at the Cloverleaf after Hannon and Perez were killed, Sperry emptied his SAW into a vehicle barreling toward the outpost. When his team examined the smoldering vehicle and the bullet-riddled bodies afterward, Sperry had killed them all. Fortunately for his state of mind, they had been four armed insurgents and not a panicking family afraid to stop at the checkpoint.

The tempo never seemed to let up, right up to November and preparations for Operation Phantom Fury, the second offensive aimed at pushing insurgents out of Fallujah. There was no time to mourn Hannon or Perez, no time to mourn whatever it was inside him that had died as well.

SPERRY'S EARLY CHILDHOOD WASN'T a war zone, but it was at times punctuated by violence, mostly at the hands of his troubled mother. His parents were divorced and Sperry spent the first eleven years of his life living with his mom, two older sisters and a younger half brother in a small farming town in Illinois—midway between Springfield and Saint Louis. His mother, Sperry says, had an explosive temper, which she mostly took out on her daughters, but sometimes on him as well.

"I remember one time," says Sperry, "sitting in the backseat of the car and I upset her by opening up a Happy Meal before we got home to find the toy for my little brother and she just lost it and turned around starting beating me up."

Sperry says on another occasion, when he was eight or nine, he can't recall why, but his mother locked him out of the house without any clothes on in the middle of winter. He stood outside in the snow banging on the door wearing only his underwear. Money was part of the problem; his mother and her second husband had a hard time supporting the family. Sperry says he remembers his mother making all the kids hide in the basement when creditors came knocking.

By the time he turned eleven, his mother's mood swings became too frequent. Sperry and his two sisters went to live with their father and his new wife in nearby Belleville, Illinois, while James's half brother stayed with his mother and her husband. The change was positive but initially unsettling for Sperry, who says he began acting out like any teenager, wearing his hair long, listening to death metal music, mouthing off to his father and his stepmom. He barely passed his classes, earning only C's and D's in school. But his rebellion lost some of its steam when his stepmother set what Sperry calls strict but fair boundaries. The confrontations tapered off even more once Sperry began seeing a therapist and after his dad introduced him to one of his own passions—golf.

Sperry quickly took to golf, enjoying the chance to bond with his father, but even more so the challenge of an individual sport where your greatest test was against yourself.

"I spent every day on the course," he says, "trying to make myself perfect." His intense focus on the sport began having a positive impact on other aspects of his life. He went from just squeaking by in school to earning A's and B's.

He won tournaments, lots of them. His father started to think that James might have had what it took to go pro. But during Sperry's junior year all that changed. The terrorist attacks of 9/11 made him believe that there was something that needed his attention more urgently than a game.

"I felt it was my generation's Pearl Harbor," Sperry says. "My generation needed to be called on to fight the people who were killing Americans. I need to do something bigger than me."

For Sperry it was that universal need to belong that J. Glenn Gray described in his book *The Warriors: Reflections on Men in Battle*: "In most of us there is a genuine longing for community with our human species, and at the same time an awkwardness and helplessness about finding the way to achieve it. Some extreme experience—mortal danger or the theatre of destruction—is necessary to bring us fully together with our comrades or with nature. This is a great pity, for there are surely alternative ways more creative and less dreadful, if men would only seek them out. Until now, war has appealed because we discover some of the mysteries of communal joy in its forbidden depths. Comradeship reaches its peak in battle."

But Sperry would also learn the cost of this kind of comradeship with the loss of so many friends during battle in Iraq.

While Sperry had an uncle who had been a Marine, his father had been in the National Guard during the Vietnam War but never deployed. He wasn't eager to see his son join up and almost certainly be sent into combat. But Sperry went to the recruiting station every day for six months until his father agreed and gave in. The compromise was he could join with an early enlistment package at seventeen but would have to finish high school before being sent off to boot camp.

There was another part of the package: Sperry's girlfriend Cathy, who would later become his wife, decided she was going to join the Marines too. They signed up the same day, hoping that they would somehow be able to stay together. They went to the same high school and had been sweethearts since freshman year. But Cathy was sent to the Marine Corps Recruit Depot at Parris Island, South Carolina, for boot camp, while Sperry was sent to other side of the country at Marine Corps Base Camp Pendleton in California to get ready to go to war.

"I was into playing video war games at the time," he tells

me as we talk, seated around the dining table of their home. "I wanted to kick in doors. My dad was mad about it. He thought I was throwing away a chance at doing something in golf to join the Marines."

While Sperry had been working out for months prior getting physically ready for Marine boot camp, he conceded he wasn't mentally ready for what the next thirteen weeks would bring. For the first three days of boot camp he felt like he was on his feet the entire time. He stood in line to get his head shaved. That first cut that made everyone the same. Then everything went to overload. The exercises they made him do pushed him beyond the endurance level of anything he had ever done before. When he was finally allowed to sleep for a few hours his body hit his rack like a rag doll, barely moving throughout the night. The mornings were like waking up in hell, the yelling, the racing to the bathrooms with some poor bastards getting too nervous to piss with the impatient lines behind them.

They could never sit; they had to either stand or squat. They would squat while cleaning their weapons until their haunches ached and finally cramped up. But they weren't denied water; in fact it was the cruel opposite. They'd have to drink so much water, chug it right down, sometimes until they puked, then they'd have to drink some more. If you screwed up, Sperry recalled, you'd find yourself doing IT, or intensive training, one-on-one with the drill instructor. This was not where you wanted to be.

After a few weeks in, Sperry felt the shock of boot camp

wearing off. He no longer felt lost. He stayed out of the drill instructors' firing lines, pushed himself hard and did what he could to help the others in his training unit. Some guys were beyond help, the mentally unstable who could hold it together through the recruiting process with the assistance of overzealous recruiting officers but quickly unraveled in boot camp. They would be dazed or paralyzed by the orders and shouting. Others would lose it altogether, Sperry said, even try to fight their own drill instructors, which was never a good idea.

"The thing that got me through," says Sperry, "is that I wanted my parents to see that I could do something on my own. I didn't want to live inside the bubble of Illinois. I wanted to be a Marine too much to not finish. I knew there would be life after boot camp."

And there was. Being a bit bigger and taller than some of the other Marines, Sperry was trained as a SAW gunner, tasked with carrying the Belgium-made M249, a gas-powered, air-cooled, $4,000, 15-pound rifle capable of delivering 750–1,000 rounds per minute. The M249 fired 5.56 x 45 NATO rounds with the accuracy of a regular rifle but with the rapid rate of fire of a machine gun. It was the center of gravity for a four-man Marine fireteam, which was built around maneuvering, protecting and utilizing its awesome firepower. The weapon provided the kind of head-bending covering fire that could keep a unit alive until they were reinforced or extricated. Despite its weight, with an added 6 pounds from a 200-round ammo box, Sperry was proud to carry it.

After boot camp, Sperry was part of one of the last waves of new Marines to join the platoon he would deploy with to Iraq within two short months, the 3rd Platoon, India Company, 3rd Battalion, 1st Marine Regiment. When Sperry finished basic and joined his platoon at another part of Camp Pendleton, the unit cohesion was already in full and ridiculous force. Guys, Sperry recalls, were strutting down a makeshift catwalk wearing boxers and body armor, one wearing nothing but camouflage paint and a canteen. It was typical Marine behavior. Despite being just weeks away from deployment to Iraq, the platoon was holding a combat fashion show, laughing in the face of the danger the entire battalion would soon face. This was, Sperry felt, exactly where he belonged.

A week before Operation Phantom Fury was set to begin, Sperry's platoon moved to an abandoned house inside the perimeter of Camp Abu Ghraib, where the rest of 3/1 was based.

Here they began an endless cycle of combat drills: entering and clearing houses, the most efficient way to remove glass from a window frame using the muzzle of an M16, how to retrieve a wounded comrade from an area with no protective cover. And then there was the checking and rechecking of gear. When someone in the platoon misplaced a thermal scope, their sergeant kept them up all night looking for it even though they were slated to move to their fighting positions just outside Fallujah the next day. It was during this countdown to the battle, Sperry says, when some Marines started suffering from unusual injuries as possible excuses to get out of fighting, like the lance corporal who accidentally shot himself in the foot with the SAW three times. Another in the unit had a sudden attack of "amnesia" after a roadside bomb incident that left him physically intact. "Where am I? Is this a gun in my hand?" Sperry imitates the Marine, shaking his head disapprovingly. There was a small respite during this period of intense training and prep for the big push when Kilo Company commandeered a passing meat truck while on patrol. It yielded enough steaks and ribs to feed hundreds of young Marines tired of T-rats and hungry for fresh meat.*

"It felt like the Last Supper," says Sperry, recalling the moment in a somewhat wistful way. Indeed, he had reason to be. At just nineteen years old he had already killed nine people in combat, lost one of his best friends and was about to go into the biggest fight of his life.

Before any battle, U.S. forces receive from the commanders the ROE orders, or rules of engagement. In this case they were given, according to Sperry, in what would be considered an unorthodox way, by a junior officer, a lieutenant from headquarters. A person none of the men recognized.

"We were basically told it was a free-fire zone," Sperry tells me. "If anything moved you were allowed to shoot it." These orders, if true, are likely the reason that Marines, dur-

---

* T-rats, or T-rations, are precooked military meals that come in rectangular tray-packs rather than individual serving sizes like MREs, or meals ready to eat. They don't need refrigeration and can feed troops in a forward operating base or combat outpost with no preparation.

ing at least three reported incidents (including the execution I witnessed), killed the prisoners they had captured, a violation of rules for prisoner treatment outlined in the Geneva Conventions.

Sperry also remembers an assembly before the battle where three-star lieutenant general James Mattis, the hard-charging, sometimes profane Marine Expeditionary Force commander, told his men that this was going to be the biggest U.S. urban military battle since the Marines fought house-to-house to dislodge five thousand North Vietnamese and Vietcong troops from Hue City during the 1968 Tet Offensive.

"What we're doing now," he remembers Mattis saying, "will be written in your child's textbooks."

Some Marines used the final hours before pushing out to write letters to their families, instructing their comrades to retrieve them under their flak jackets if they were to fall. Sperry was not one of them. "I didn't even want to think about that or talk about it," he says.

At the company level the battle plan was for Kilo Company to push the insurgents south and for India Company to flank them in a pincer movement and simply kill them. It would, like Hue City, be house-to-house fighting with plans, Sperry was told, to clear every single house. In reality, the Marines would not go into a house until they had contact, meaning someone was shooting at them. At three A.M. on November 8, 2004, India Company moved to its fighting position north of the Fallujah railway station. They were "welcomed" to the area with an insurgent round fired from an RPG, which hit one of the trucks but didn't explode.

THE MEN DUG PROTECTIVE trenches around their vehicles and slept, exhausted, for much of the next day and night as jets and artillery began softening up the city for the ground assault to come.

When the order finally came to move, Sperry was surprised at how empty the city was. It seemed to him like a ghost town. At first, as the Marines entered, they found no insurgents but fully loaded weapons staged behind walls and other tactical locations. Sperry picked up an AK-47 lying on the ground, stripped off its banana clip and ejected the 7.62 round already in the chamber before dropping it back down. "Dumbass," someone yelled at him, "that coulda been booby-trapped."

While the Marines of Sperry's 3rd Platoon still couldn't see them, the insurgents let them know they hadn't completely left town. Lance Corporal Jody Perrite got hit with a sniper round in his right arm, which entered right below his Marine bulldog tattoo and exited on the other side. Other Marines started getting picked off too. The insurgents were prepared and knew the terrain. They used low-tech improvisational tactics to safeguard their firing positions, like scattering shards of broken lightbulbs on the concrete stairways leading to the rooftops where they were hiding. That way when the Marines moved in they'd hear them coming. The confusion and uncertainty of combat also gave way to comic moments. As Sperry and his squad moved up the stairway of one house, the squad lined up outside a closed door made from corrugated aluminum. Believing there were insurgents on the rooftop, the Marine in front, carrying a shotgun, wound up and stomp-kicked the door, center-mass. Instead of caving in, it reverberated like a cymbal back on the kicker in a loud twang. The Marines laughed, knowing that any element of surprise was just lost with their clumsy entrance. The rooftop was clear, but the Marines started taking fire from the roof of another location. They ducked behind the parapet. A Marine in the squad put his Kevlar helmet on the muzzle of his M16 and poked it high enough to draw fire from the snipers. When they saw where the shots were coming from, the fireteam leader fired a 40 mm grenade from the M203 grenade launcher slung under his rifle. After the explosion, the rooftop went silent. But the calm didn't last very long. The snipers were just the trigger for an insurgent trap in the normally busy market area known as Jolan Park. Once the Marines entered the maze of narrow alleyways, they got boxed in by sniper fire in front of them and RPG rounds to the rear. And now that they had the Marines where they wanted them, insurgents began hanging mortar rounds right on top of them. The illusion of an abandoned Fallujah had just gone to shit. The trapped Marines called up the heavy guns.

Abrams M1A1 tanks rumbled down the wider passageways, rotating their turrets to the left or the right like iron elephants deciding whether to charge. Once the turret swiveled in the direction of a target, a car parked in an alleyway or even a

suspicious container, it wasn't long before the tank's main gun
punched a high-explosive round into it, turning the target into
a ball of flame.

Sperry was told by his team leader to move up the street
and get in front and to the right of one of the tanks to provide security. "Fuck no," he remembers telling him. There
wasn't any cover up there. But Sperry said he soon relented and
within moments of taking his position, he found himself swirl-
ing down the rabbit hole that would change his life forever.

"The next thing I know I'm smelling gunpowder. I didn't
hear anything but remember the sensation of me being thrown
on my back," says Sperry. "Then I black out and when I wake
up, Doc Jacoby is working on me. 'Holy shit, look at his Kevlar,' I remember somebody saying. Then Sergeant Love said to
me, 'Hold on, Sperry, for your wife. You're going to be okay.'
Then I looked up and remember seeing you taking pictures of
me and then I blacked out again."

Sitting in his home, seated around this table with him and
his wife, I'm fascinated, finally hearing the details I never knew
from our encounter so many years ago in Fallujah. For me,
Sperry was the first American casualty I saw during the fight
for Fallujah. I remember following a group of Marines carrying him into the cover of an alleyway after he was wounded,
Hannon's rosary dangling from his belt loop. Several men
propped him up while the Navy corpsman bandaged his head.
"I remember being stretchered out," he says. "I wake up again,
on the chopper, puking blood straight up, and it was falling
down on my face. I turn to my left and there are body bags in

the middle of the Chinook.* The doc [a medic] wipes blood off my eyes. Then I don't remember anything until being at Balad in a tent and some guys were checking me out.† A female nurse, a brunette, asks me how I'm doing. My head hurts. I'm taken for scan. I black out again. The most I can remember from Balad is that brunette nurse taking care of me."

After his flight to Germany, Sperry woke up in a hospital room filled with three wounded officers all on life support. When a nurse came in and called him Captain Sperry, even given his head injuries he still realized there had been a mix-up in admissions. It didn't take long for him to be moved to the enlisted ranks area of the hospital. But the confusion didn't end there. Sperry had been reported KIA, or killed in action, by someone from his battalion. Fortunately for his family, that information never reached them. Sperry was able to call his father and stepmother from the hospital. They weren't at home at the time, but he was able to leave a voice mail letting them know he had been injured but was still alive and in Germany. Cathy, however, was still at Camp Lejeune, in generator-repair school, and learned of his injury from my report before anyone

---

* The CH-47 Chinook is an American heavy-lift, double-rotor transport helicopter. It has been in continual use by the U.S. military since the Vietnam War.

† Balad, seventy miles north of Baghdad, was a hub site of air operations both under former dictator Saddam Hussein and for coalition forces following the U.S.-led invasion of Iraq. Under the U.S. military occupation it became known as Joint Base Balad.

officially notified her. The combat images I transmitted from my laptop and satellite modem from the battlefield were grainy and dark, but Cathy says she knew with one look and without any doubt that the wounded Marine whose head was being bandaged in front of my camera was her husband, James.

What injured Sperry is still a mystery even now. Fellow Marines suspected it was a bullet ricochet, while his doctors in Germany believe it may have been a tiny fragment of a rocket-propelled grenade that sliced through his Kevlar helmet and into his brain. Whatever it was, it took out a sliver of his frontal lobe, the part of the brain that controls emotions and is also said to be the place where our personality resides. Sperry had a litany of injuries in addition to the mystery trauma to his brain. This includes fractures at the base of his skull and his nose, as well as a broken sternum and four broken ribs caused by the force of shrapnel or bullet rounds blunted by the ceramic plate inserted at the front of his body armor. Doctors pumped him full of steroids to counter the cranial pressure of his brain bleed and stabilized him enough to fly him back to the U.S. While he waited for the transport, Sperry says, he got bored, rolled his wheelchair across the street to a PX and bought a six-pack of Bud Light. Though still on morphine for his pain, he says he savored one of the beers, his first in months, until an orderly took the rest away.

On the flight from Germany to a hospital in California, Sperry's jet stopped at Scott Air Force Base in Saint Louis, where his dad and his stepmother were able to see him during a short layover. He had asked them in an earlier telephone call to find out what had happened to other members of his unit, since he'd had little to no contact with anyone since being flown out of Fallujah. During the Saint Louis layover, his father gave him a sheet of paper. On it was a list of twenty names, all Marines from Sperry's unit who had not made it out of Fallujah alive.* Sperry says he dropped the paper and put his face in his hands, wondering how that was even possible.

But after Sperry was admitted to Balboa naval hospital in San Diego, he discovered that he might have lost more than his friends. When his wife, Cathy, first came to see him in his hospital ward, after months of painful separation, something strange happened. For Sperry there was no overwhelming sense of relief to see her again, no joyful reunion. In fact, no feelings at all. Sperry says it was as if he were just seeing any other friend for a night of pizza or bowling. I look at Cathy's face while he says this, but there's no expression. In the time since, perhaps she's come to feel the same about him. I look at them both and wonder if Sperry's head injury has also impacted his capacity to feel.

Sperry and Cathy spent the next two years at Pendleton on a seesaw teetering between hope and despair. Too often, despair seemed to have the greater mass. While Cathy would go to work on base, Sperry spent his days, by his own admis-

---

* According to U.S. Marine Corps documents, 3/1 Marines had the highest casualty rate of any unit during Operation Phantom Fury, with 22 killed and 206 wounded in action.

sion, drinking with another wounded Marine from his unit from sunup to sundown or whenever they passed out.

"We went about our separate ways," says Cathy of those times. "He would go with Phil drinking day and night. It was a losing battle for me so I just gave in to him." And while Cathy gave in to him, Sperry gave in to a recklessness that defied his own mortality, manifesting itself in a series of "crotch rocket" high-performance motorcycles.

Sperry, wasted on tequila sunrises, would take his bikes out riding around, popping wheelies at seventy miles per hour. On one occasion, he says he took his Italian Aprilia out on the freeway and pushed it to a hundred and sixty miles per hour while completely drunk. He took a deep breath afterward and realized exactly how close he had come to crossing that line between obliviousness and oblivion. He sold the bike two weeks later to keep himself from doing it again. The sale, however, did not stop his drinking.

"I didn't cry for two years," Sperry says. "I drank all my sorrows away." Or he tried to. It became a choice between the pain, the splitting migraines from the physical and emotional trauma of his combat experiences, and the puking and massive hangovers from his daily drinking. The strains on his marriage were becoming intractable.

"It was kind of a blur," Cathy says of the time. "I was so young, I didn't know how to help him."

"I wanted her to understand what I was going through." Sperry says, nodding, as we continue talking around the table. "She couldn't see it."

The strain did not prevent Cathy from becoming pregnant and on July 12, 2006, their daughter, Hannah, was born. Sperry named her after his best friend killed in Iraq, Fernando Hannon. Although Hannah's birth provided some sense of hope for him, it was not enough to lift the darkness that surrounded him. The gravity of the deaths of nearly two dozen of his Marine friends in Iraq was crushing him. He saw their faces every day, remembered how they messed with each other but how when it came down to the fighting, they always had each other's backs. The band-of-brothers cliché was true, he knew it, but what was also true was that in combat you had so little control. No matter how hard you look, how do you see a roadside bomb before it blows? How do you stop a sniper's bullet before it hits? Even as your brothers watch out for you and you watch out for them, these things are beyond your control, especially when you're fighting phantoms like the insurgents who rarely show themselves in Iraq. While he drank to forget, the booze wasn't enough. It couldn't dull, let alone blot out, the physical and emotional pain he endured every day, the migraines, the backaches, the insomnia. On September 6, 2006, nearly two years after he was wounded in Fallujah, it all became too much.

"I remember it started out normal," says Sperry. "I'm not sure what triggered it, but I think I had a flashback. I was thinking how I lost so many friends and was missing them so much." And the alcohol only made things worse. That morning, in the garage of his house on base, Sperry threw a rope over the end of one of the support beams just as a gunnery sergeant neighbor, also back from Iraq, had done down the street only a few weeks earlier. At that moment nothing good was getting through a brain damaged by shrapnel, muddled by alcohol and wracked by survivor's guilt. Sperry doesn't know how long he stood there wondering if making the noose would be his point of no return. Is this how he wanted to go out? Dangling at the end of a rope in his garage where his wife would find him and never be able to erase the image from her mind? Sperry stopped. He yanked the rope back down, got into his car and drove to the VA (Veterans Affairs) outreach center on the base. When he arrived, he says, there were three men ahead of him. He sat in his car in the parking lot, staring ahead and blasting the stereo until someone came out to talk with him.

They said he "sounded like a robot," Sperry says, when he answered questions from the counselor who came out to check on him. The counselor realized Sperry was suicidal. He called a police escort and Sperry was taken to the VA's mental health facility in San Diego. He spent the next few hours in a padded room talking to a psychiatrist, who decided to commit him for his own safety. They stripped him of all his clothes and belongings, anything with which he could hurt himself, and moved him into the facility for the next two weeks.

While Sperry pulled himself back from the brink, hundreds of others who served in the wars in Iraq and Afghanistan did not. In fact, U.S. Department of Veterans Affairs secretary Eric Shinseki announced that out of the thirty thousand suicides in America each year, a full 20 percent are committed by veterans. The Department of Defense's Suicide Event Report, a compilation of suicide information and analysis across all branches of the military, notes that eleven hundred service members killed themselves in the four years from 2005–2009, or one suicide every thirty-six hours.

During my research, psychiatrist Dr. Jonathan Shay told me that suicide was a commonplace thought amongst the mostly Vietnam-era veterans he worked with as staff psychiatrist in the VA outpatient clinic in Boston. "Almost everyone thinks daily of suicide," he said. "It seems to sustain them as a bottom line of human freedom and dignity. Having touched that talisman every day, they continue to struggle."

BUT DURING HIS TIME in the VA mental health facility in San Diego two things happened for Sperry: first, he had some time to detox from all the alcohol he had been drowning himself in for the last two years, and second, he was exposed to Vietnam War veterans who provided both positive and negative reinforcements toward reshaping his life. He could see within the VA hospital how self-medicating, mostly with alcohol, had utterly destroyed so many of these men. The memories of their war had ravaged them so completely that they spent the rest of their days toasting to their own demise. They were little more than carcasses now, men who most likely would've preferred to die during their deployments, rather than the slow postwar attrition that killed them from the inside out. The Vietnam vets who had kicked the booze told him as much, that being sober was the only way he was likely to survive.

He could see their point and realized that at the very least, he had to cut back on the drinking or he could really end up swinging from the roof beam of his own garage. But giving up drinking without something to replace it wasn't an option Sperry was ready to try. So the memories that he had once tried to wash away he was now determined to blow up in smoke.

But he also knew he needed to make other changes. Camp Pendleton had become a neighborhood of bad influences, where other damaged Marines, returning from Iraq and Afghanistan, pursued self-destructive trajectories. Sperry had to break away from that to truly heal. Home sounded safe, and being in a safe place was becoming critically important to him. In October 2007, Sperry, Cathy and Hannah moved back to his father's house in Illinois. They stayed for six months and things seemed to improve. In April 2008 they rented their own home, and that's where things turned dark again. That sense of safety, of being around family, someone watching your back, evaporated in their new surroundings. Sperry never slept. His nights and days began to blend together, punctuated only by the anger and restlessness that had him punching holes in the walls. Despite the fragile physical condition of his skull, where any kind of blow had the potential to cause permanent brain damage or kill him, Sperry found his anger spilling over to human targets. A small provocation led him to pounce on a young man in the parking lot of a Walmart.

And he tells me about the night in which he nearly killed a man. Unable to sleep, Sperry had been sitting up watching television when he heard something slam into his house. When he went to investigate he saw a man walking up to his door. Sperry immediately sprang toward the man, tackled him and held the knife he always carried over the man's heart.

"I could've plunged it in him at any moment," Sperry says, recalling the incident. But then the guy pointed toward a black cylinder in the yard. His tire. He had been making a turn on Sperry's street when it came off the rim and rolled against the door of Sperry's house. He had simply come to retrieve it. What he found instead was an enraged ex-Marine intent on keeping his security perimeter from being breached.

Sperry released his grip on the man's shirt and sat back on the grass. The man grabbed the tire and sped off into the night on three tires and a rim shedding sparks. Sperry sat there—he can't remember how long, maybe a few minutes or maybe a few hours—wondering what had happened to him, how every noise and movement had become a threat to him and his family.

Now, back here in this place, Sperry gets up from the dining room table, goes to the cupboard and gets the ingredients he needs to make Hannah a peanut butter and jelly sandwich. He does this while telling me all the drugs he still has in his medicine cabinet, the stuff he needs to take daily just to function. Cathy sits quietly, uncomfortable. It took a long time for all of us to get here, to be sitting around his kitchen table talking. Tracking him down was a perpetual challenge. Then he would pop up on my e-mail or in a text message. There was always some kind of crazy excuse that told me he was still struggling: a car accident where he got T-boned and the phone was destroyed, the dog chewed the phone charger, and then he texted me one day to say he couldn't make our telephone interview that day because his mother had died. That was true, as true as any of the other excuses may have been as well. His mother, with whom he always had a strained relationship, with a few exceptions, had contracted flulike symptoms and within a few days was dead. Sperry explained it to me later as "some kind of complications from the swine flu." I asked if there were drugs or alcohol involved and he said he didn't think so, but that she had had a hard life and he wanted to leave it at that. He said that he had forgiven her in the end and that she had learned from her child-rearing mistakes with him and his sisters and had given his younger half brother a wonderful childhood, filling him with goals and aspirations. During that time after his mother died, he understandably disappeared for nearly a month before we talked again.

As we sit at the Sperrys' kitchen table, there are moments when the conversation is fluid and we laugh and moments when I feel I'm providing some value to both of them, closing some time or informational gaps by showing them the video of his injury in battle. But there are other moments when I feel I am just a reminder of the beginning of his fall, just an annoyance that everyone, even the dog, wishes would leave.

But everything we talked about, all the ponderings of the past, seems to have led up to this one powerful and uncomfortable truth: Sperry says he no longer feels love, not for his wife, nor—as he looks at Hannah pressing Play-Doh into the table—his beautiful blond-haired daughter.

Whether it was the small piece of metal that pierced his

skull, slicing into his left frontal lobe and excising the very bit we insist makes us human, or the cumulative toll of all he had to see and do in his war, James Sperry says he cannot feel love.

"I felt love before," he says insistently, "but now I just feel numb."

He said as much to the local newspapers when they asked him about his injuries when he first came home. "I don't love my wife," he told them, though he didn't mean for it to sound as cold as it did. She wasn't at all happy about that, he admits. Cathy looks at him as though she's considered these words so many times before and has come to peace with them.

"He's going to need therapy to feel those emotions," she says with a shrug. "I'd like to see him do more therapy," she says. "When he actually seems happy it's just stoned happy, it's not real happiness." But Sperry has resisted counseling, feeling that nothing more can be done.

"I can tell them how much I miss my friends and cry like it's a confessional," Sperry says, defending himself. "But I feel there's nothing a doctor can tell me that's going to reboot that part of my brain."

I point to Hannah. "But do you feel the way other fathers feel about their daughters? Do you love her?"

"She's my responsibility," he says matter-of-factly. "I have to be there for her, but there's no warm and fuzzy, no tingles."

Sperry says he knows things will always be different, but he believes there's still some type of life out there for him. He had wanted to go into law enforcement after the Marines, but his cognitive abilities have been so severely diminished he knows he won't qualify. Standardized tests he's taken since returning from war show him in the bottom percentiles. He tried going to school when he came home but just couldn't concentrate. He used to be smart, he says, and now he just doesn't know who he is.

He also still has nightmares, wrapping past and present together in fearful imagery. In one, he's driving the family car loaded with Hannah, the dogs and his sister's children down Fallujah's treacherous streets.

He thinks he can stay stable if he stays on his medications, doesn't return to heavy drinking, learns a trade and raises his daughter. He likes spending time with his daughter and his sister's children, making them lunches, taking them to and from school.

"Children are innocent. They don't know the cruelties of the war."

"Will you tell her your stories one day?" I ask.

"She knows Daddy was a Marine," he says. "That's all the stories she probably needs to know about that."

Sperry knows his own innocence was lost in war.

"I was so young and naïve. I'm in high school playing video games, but at seventeen you don't really know what happens. We're fearless at that age, but now [after war] we become petrified of death. Everyone I've been with [in Iraq] has been killed themselves or are now really messed up."

In *The Warriors*, J. Glenn Gray wrote that the only way some soldiers, like Sperry, lose this naïveté is through their own physical injury. "In most of these soldiers, the sources of their relationship toward death—as a reality for others only—is not too difficult to discover. They have simply preserved their childish illusion that they are the center of the world and are therefore immortal . . . Perhaps their own wounding is necessary. The look of shock and outrage on such a soldier's face when that happens is likely to be unforgettable. At one cruel stroke he loses forever the faith in his physical immortality. His psychological adjustment to the new world he has to inhabit is certain to be harder than the physical recovery from his wounds."

After our Christmas meeting, my correspondence with Sperry over the next year is sporadic and shows his significant mood swings, likely from continued drug and alcohol use. I'm familiar with this, recognizing the chemically induced patterns of emotional highs and lows in myself. In some e-mails he seems helpless, in others defiant.

February 21, 2010 (e-mail from Sperry to me)
Sorry I have been really struggling with all my demons lately. I keep numbing myself up with weed, pills, and alcohol. I have been thinking about trying to tell the doctors at my next Marine Corps. doctor evaluation that I am totally fine and trying to release me. I was a great saw gunner and they need my talents over there. I hate being on the sidelines watching other boys and men fight this war. I can walk and pull my trigger finger. I think I am addicted to combat. Sorry for all the delay i have been numbing myself pretty good and trying to

*forget about how fucked up this world is. I want to be
there for you as well I know you know the same pain.
How do you cope with pain and mind-racing? I think
I might check myself back in a VA hospital but if i do
that there go my chances of the army. I hate being on the
sidelines, I use to be important now everyone takes me
for granted. I am so lost. . . . . .Peace*

September 14, 2010 (Facebook message from Sperry to me)

*Well lets get right back into it. I have time to
contemplate everything in depth lately. The man that
was James before everything—was motivated, naive,
full of hope, and had innocence. I just feel like that
man died over there and I am stuck with an existence
that does not feel—it just calculates everything, the
risk of going out in public, numb to any emotion I act
emotions out so people think I am somewhat fine. But
I haven't felt them then unless I am going 160 mph on a
crotch rocket . . . I am told why are you not seeing your
doctors? What are they going to do for me? They are not
going to understand at all what I am going thru from
the constant pains in my head, upper back, and hips,
knees, feet. To not sleeping for days, nightmares, lack of
feeling anything but anger, flashbacks, breaking down
at the drop of a hat. To asking why did I lose twenty-
six friends and I am still here. I constantly contemplate
what the last few seconds for my friends were [like].*

What were they feeling? I contemplate my death daily.
Also my daughters. When I look at people I try not to,
but I picture what they would look like dead. I smoke
pot non-stop just to keep me from exploding. It calms
me down. I think that if suicidal veterans would receive
pot for PTSD it would calm them down and help them
think things out. I have almost died so many times, I
can't even count. . . . I don't know what to do anymore.
Giving up is not an option. I am not a quitter.

LATER, I LEARN THROUGH Facebook postings that Sperry has separated from his wife, Cathy. I'm not surprised. The challenges to their relationship seemed nearly insurmountable. Cathy told me that the effect of Sperry's drinking and multiple medications had left her feeling isolated and alone. There were also the occasions, she said, when he was verbally abusive and his explosive temper sometimes made her fear for the safety of her daughter and herself. I ask her about it. It takes her a few weeks to respond, but finally I receive this:

December 29, 2010 (Facebook message from Cathy to me)
Hi Kevin, I'm sorry, I didn't mean to blow you off. It's
just that it's been easier to just push my feelings aside
and not think about it. And to be honest it does make
me a little nervous having so many personal details out
there. As far as our marriage, I feel like we are done.

It hurts me to see him in pain and I really hope that he gets help and finds happiness, mostly for Hannah's sake. I care about him and his well-being, but our marriage lacked passion for years. Maybe I am being selfish, but I feel like for years he put me down and I started to believe it and it turned me into a person I didn't like. Maybe it was because of his own insecurities that he knew he was weak inside and was afraid of me being strong. But for the first time in my life I feel strong and independent. I feel like him and I brought out the worst in each other, some of it Iraq is to blame, but also at 19, we didn't know how to be married and never truly respected each other. One example of this is, he got a motorcycle loan without talking to me first, and I got a credit card without telling him . . . we just started bad habits like that from the beginning. He is leaving this week to go to a rehab center out of state and I am very happy he is finally going to get help. I want to see him get better and I will always care about him, and I do feel sad for what has become of us. But, my feelings have changed for him, and it wouldn't be fair to either of us to stay together. We have so many different views on everything and are not the same people we married. And I don't feel like we are capable of being what each other wants in a mate. I do enjoy the freedom of being able to figure out who I am without someone standing in my way and I feel like I am a stronger person than I was then when we were together.

Shortly after, I see on Facebook that Cathy has changed back to her maiden name.

At the same time I e-mailed Cathy, I had also sent James a note asking him if he thinks his marriage was a casualty of his war injuries and PTSD and whether there are behaviors he wishes he could change.

He writes me back through Facebook, responding thoughtfully and candidly.

December 14, 2010 (Facebook message from Sperry to me)

I really do not like being away from Cathy because she was always that rock for me, but with all the stress that of the whole experience, I just was not the same confident person anymore I became very selfish, mood swings, and numb to any emotion. Unfortunately, I said and did so many bad things. There wasn't a name in the book that I didn't call her. I was just angry and violent. Then I found pot. This helped a ton into relaxing me and thinking through situations before I would fly off the handle. But the negatives that have come with it were the smell of it and me. Cathy saw that it helped me and wanted me to have it. During this time it was almost daily war between us. We both didn't care what we said to each other. We hurt each other a lot. But it got to a point that we would yell at each other so much that a brick wall just went up in our mind to what each other was trying to say. There

were also very beautiful times and great times that we
all had together. From group parties to beach days.
Not all of it was yelling and fighting there were some
great days in there. My anger was extreme I regret
that more then anything I am deeply and truly sorry
to Cathy for all that I put her threw emotionally. She
is a very different person now she is very resourceful
and strong willed. But at least in my presence I don't
see the passion she used to have for me or her art or
photography. I miss that more then anything she was
a very bubbly person around me and I have not seen
her truly happy in years. I am sure other people have
but not me. She use to love me so much that nothing
would have broken it but war did and the way I
handled all the pain I have had to endure from weekly
migraines and vomiting so much that my teeth are
thinning out and decaying, to my hips, shoulders, chest
and knee to all the emotional trauma that lost of so
many friends. My whole world-view has changed to
one of utter disgust of the human kind. Not the people
trying to get by, but the hierarchy that rule and exploit
the world. I am extremely afraid and depressed of what
will be left of this earth for my daughter. I still live in
the house you visited. Cathy is living a half hour away.
I try and see Hannah three days a week. She is why
I'm trying to get better. I am going to go to a in patient
treatment center in Georgia called the Shepherd
Center. I need to do this for myself. How have you

been Kevin? Hannah asks about you everyone once in
a while. She still sleeps every night with the panda you
got her.

By January, I get a message from Sperry that he has
checked himself into the Shepherd Center in Atlanta, Georgia,
as he said he would. The Shepherd Center is a not-for-profit
hospital that specializes in research, treatment and rehabilitation for people with spinal cord and brain injury. Sperry seems
a perfect candidate and seems upbeat about the prospects for
himself.

A MONTH LATER, HE sends me another note about the center's
holistic approach to treating post-traumatic stress and traumatic brain injury, which seems to mix the healing philoso-
phies of both East and West.

> **February 2011 (Facebook message from Sperry to me)**
> *The treatment has been great. They work on every aspect*
> *of your problems. They educate you on what happens*
> *to your brain after TBI (Traumatic Brain Injury) and*
> *PTSD. Then you have groups on PTSD, adjustment to*
> *civilian life, cognitive functions, controlling anger. They*
> *have a physical therapist that works on whatever ever*
> *hurts and explores why and how to treat or strengthen.*
> *They have a warrior life coach that shows you how to*
> *change your thought process. Then you have doctors that*

just work on pain management and general care. They
aso do funcitonal life skills, yoga, tai chi, acupuncture—
just about everything.

I think about everything that James Sperry has been
through and how he first wrote me during the middle of his
own debilitating physical pain and mental chaos. Despite his
embittered state, his feelings of being damaged, worthless and
guilty for just being alive, he was still able to reach out to me
with comfort for my own battlefield guilt. He's also shared
with me the real-time narrative of his own healing. For all his
wounds and the horrors he's experienced, I see the warrior
still, a man whose humanity abides. Recognizing my small
efforts on his behalf years ago, he returned the favor with an
offer of redemption, helping protect me from what he knew
to be the most unforgiving postwar enemy, ourselves. I smile
when I see this self-portrait he posted on Facebook at the
end of his treatment. The caption reads simply, "New and
improved James."

"New and improved James"—James Sperry's
profile picture on Facebook, May 12, 2011

POSTSCRIPT

James is now a mentor with the Wounded Warrior Regiment and travels around the country helping other veterans
to get treatment. After learning of his ordeal, President and
Mrs. Obama invited James, Hannah and Cathy for a visit to
the White House.

James Sperry and Hannah with the president and his wife

Gunnery Sergeant Leonard Shelton, U.S.M.C. (on left)
3rd Battalion, 5th Marines
The Gulf War (1991)

CHAPTER 4

SOMEONE'S NOT LISTENING

*After that battle everything was pretty foggy. I stopped
praying, I grew up in a Christian environment. But I
didn't believe it anymore. Human flesh melting on steel?*

THE EVIDENCE was mounting, but Marine Sergeant Leonard Shelton still didn't believe he would actually go to war. He didn't want to believe it. His unit was already deployed in the baking sands of the Saudi Arabian desert, the first potential combat deployment for the light armored infantry battalion that had just been activated six years earlier in 1985. Their LAV-25s were amphibious, eight-wheeled rapid-transit personnel carriers with a maximum speed of sixty miles per hour and were topped with a 25 mm cannon. They operated with a crew of three and could transport four to six Marines. Even though he was the commander of one of the LAV-25s, Shelton had never been in real combat before and was not prepared for what he was about to encounter.

"We were being kind of lazy in the back of the vehicles,

trying to hide from the sun," he says. "We weren't taking it seriously. Our behavior showed we weren't taking it seriously."

Like all soldiers with time on their hands they would goof on each other mercilessly but then share stories about their homes and families. Shelton, a black kid from Cleveland, Ohio, says he joined the military as a way to escape a personal sense of confusion from events he suffered as a child—sexual abuse, he claimed, by a member of his own extended family. While the Marines weren't a completely natural fit for him, he found they provided him with purpose and direction. He also found camaraderie and friendship with young men from places he likely would've never been exposed to. One of them was a lance corporal named Thomas Jenkins from the historical gold-mining town of Mariposa, California. Jenkins's family was of pioneer stock. Jenkins himself was trained as an EMT and spent the summers fighting fires for the U.S. Forest Service.

Shelton says that when they were first training on the LAVs he and Jenkins would sometimes race their vehicles against each other when no one was watching. Their shenanigans continued in Saudi Arabia for a time. But then Alpha Company commander Captain Michael Schupp saw what was happening and gathered his men together.

"He put us in a *school circle*. He actually talked to us and didn't yell at us," says Shelton. "He talked to us like human beings, like Marines. 'I want to bring us all home and I need your help,' he told us. The look in his eyes of his concern and care, his sincerity, changed everything for me. We had to depend on each other."

It wasn't long before Shelton and his unit got to see the real face of war. It would be the first actual ground engagement of the Gulf War, the culmination of a coalition air campaign that had begun twenty-two days earlier. Shelton's light armored infantry battalion, operating under the designation Task Force Shepherd, was dug in near the Kuwaiti border. They were miles ahead of the main fighting task force and their role was to be a trip wire of sorts, both an early warning and early challenge to any advancing Iraqi forces. On January 29, 1991, elements of three Iraqi divisions, two infantry and one tank, crossed the border into Saudi Arabia from Kuwait in a large attack designed to draw coalition forces into a ground battle. The movement triggered the American Marine recon teams and LAV units, which scattered along the border.

"This is the first time we were engaging in combat," says Shelton. "There was lots of confusion, lots of firepower, lots of fog. The first engagement started at dusk when we were fired on by Iraqi tanks."

The primary fighting took place along a perimeter the coalition forces called Observation Post 4. While Shelton's LAV could lay down harassing fire, its 25 mm chain gun had little chance of penetrating the hulls of the Iraqi T-55 and T-72 main battle tanks.

"It was crazy, man, when we got the air support in and we were shooting at tanks, trying to hit their view box, but we didn't get up and personal until they were all destroyed," he says.

Shelton's unit was reinforced in the rear by platoons of

LAV-ATs, similar to LAV-25s, but with mounted TOW anti-tank missiles as their primary weapons instead of 25 mm chain guns. These could actually take out the Iraqi tanks once they were in range. At one point during the fighting Shelton heard an explosion from behind. At first, he and others thought that the Iraqi forces may have penetrated their lines and were now firing behind them. What had actually happened was that one of the reinforcing LAV-ATs spotted what they thought was an Iraqi tank within the American lines and requested permission to fire their TOW missile. The missile cleared its tube and found its target with a tremendous explosion. But the TOW hadn't hit an Iraqi tank. It hit another American LAV-AT a few hundred meters ahead of them. The missile penetrated the rear hatch of the LAV designated "Green Two," detonating its supply of more than a dozen missiles stored in the rear. Eyewitnesses say it erupted into a tremendous fireball, instantly killing all four crewmembers, including Green Two's commander, Corporal Ismael Cotto. Cotto, twenty-seven, was a smart Puerto Rican kid from the South Bronx who had defied the odds of his poor neighborhood by not only graduating from high school but also attending college for three years, before fulfilling his dream of enlisting in the Marines. Shelton knew him from their time being deployed together.

The mistakes and confusion of that early engagement only seemed to get worse. A few hours into the fight, coalition forces began receiving air support from American A-10 Thunderbolts.* But the planes had difficulty locating Iraqi tanks within the lines and began dropping flares over the battleground to provide illumination. One of the flares landed near an American LAV-25, Red Two. After-action reports indicate that the Red Two's vehicle commander attempted to identify himself as a "friendly," but that didn't prevent one of the A-10s from firing an AGM-65 air-to-ground missile, which destroyed the LAV and killed all of its crew with the exception of the driver, who was ejected from the vehicle. An after-battle investigation by the Marines suggested that a malfunctioning missile, rather than human error, caused the incident. Regardless, the end result was that seven more Marines were dead at the hands of their own forces, including Shelton's friend Lance Corporal Thomas Jenkins.† Together, the incidents resulted in eleven of the first American deaths in the Gulf ground war—all of them from inaptly named "friendly fire."

It wouldn't be until daybreak, after the initial fighting ended, that Shelton would learn of what happened to Jenkins

---

* The A-10 Thunderbolt is an American military jet developed in the 1970s to provide close air support to ground combat troops. Because it was neither sleek looking nor fast it was nicknamed the Warthog, but armed with a 30 mm cannon and air-to-ground missiles, it was particularly deadly during the Gulf War, reportedly destroying nearly one thousand Iraqi tanks and thousands of other military vehicles and artillery pieces.

† Because the eleven American deaths came so early in the Gulf War's ground combat operations and were considered "friendly fire," Jenkins's photo was featured on the February 18, 1991, cover of *Time* with the title "The War Comes Home."

and Cotto, that his friends had been killed not at the hands of the Iraqis but rather by their own troops. But American commanders didn't have time to deconstruct the mistakes that led to the killing of their own men. During that first battle, the Iraqis had captured and occupied the border town of al-Khafji. What the Iraqi troops didn't realize, however, was that a handful of recon Marines were still hiding inside some of the buildings when the town was captured. These Marines would stay in their hiding spots, undiscovered, and would later help coordinate a counterattack from within, by directing A-10s to strike against Iraqi tanks around al-Khafji.

Shelton's forces helped support the counterattack the next day, providing fire support for advancing Saudi and Qatari troops, who were part of the American-led coalition brought together to oust the Iraqis after their invasion and occupation of Kuwait. But when Shelton's 25 mm chain gun jammed, his platoon leader ordered Shelton's vehicle to pull back and assist the company gunnery sergeant Leroy Ford in the rear. Shelton says that's when he saw the images that he would never be able to clear from his mind.

"When I got off the vehicle I asked Gunny Ford, 'What do you need?' He had his back against the gate of the Humvee. I looked to the left and the poncho had flown off the bodies with a gust of wind, and that's when I went into shock. Jenkins was lying there completely burnt. His body was completely charred. All I could see were the whites of his teeth. I knew it was him because the gunny had already labeled . . . he had a tag on his boots. I also noticed that it was their vehicle. Right then I got into a state of shock, I couldn't speak, I couldn't talk, this was a blow that was more real than I could ever imagine. I fell to my knees, I looked at him [Gunny Ford] to help me with my feelings. Nothing."

Nearly twenty years later Shelton is still overcome with the imagery, just as vivid and real as if he were looking at it now. After he tells me the story, he begins weeping, inconsolably, into the phone. I begin to realize what a risk I've been taking in asking these soldiers and Marines to take me back to their most difficult moments, to relive their most painful memories of war. While I might be able to get them to take me there, I wonder, while listening to Shelton's grief, if sharing their war stories might have the unintended consequence of making things worse.

"It could've been the confusion, or the rage, but I kept shouting they were dead and 'I don't want to do this shit anymore.' I was angry and confused. I thought [the platoon leader] had set me up to see the bodies," says Shelton, sobbing.

"But when I was walking back to my vehicle, he's actually trying to calm me down, trying to get me to refocus. It was in a gentle way. Still, I didn't want them touching me, I didn't want them around me. Because they didn't see what I saw," he says insistently. "They couldn't tell me that it was going to be all right, because there wasn't anything anyone could say. They couldn't tell me anything that would fix what I had experienced. I just wanted to be left the fuck alone. I was shocked. I was in shock, man. I remember getting back on the vehicle after I saw them on the desert floor. I looked at my gunner and the lieutenant was on radio; I hadn't responded for five to thirty minutes. He kept calling me on the radio and I couldn't speak. I'm looking at my gunner and he says to me, 'Can you please say something to him please?' Finally, I say over the radio, 'They're dead, they're dead, they're all dead!' "

Shelton pauses and after what seems like several minutes, he continues. "At first there was silence," Shelton says, "then you hear back over the radio, 'Calm down, Blue 2 [Shelton's radio call sign], calm down.' I could tell my gunner was afraid. But I didn't want it, I didn't want to hear what he had to say. We never even talked about it for the whole time. It hurt too damn much. I didn't feel a sense of fear of running away, just rage. The initial shock of death, it was more than rage. I never want to feel that way again. It was animalistic. I never want to feel that way again. You get angry and want to kill. The rage is just incredible. Then we got back into the fight. We were just firing at everything. God, man, I never knew who they were [the Iraqi soldiers]. I didn't know who they were—who the fuck are these people?

"After the fighting was done I was so exhausted. It was like something was gone in me. It was like part of something was gone. This was my world; there was nothing else. After that battle everything was pretty foggy. I stopped praying; I grew up in a Christian environment, but I didn't believe it anymore. Human flesh melting on steel? Someone's not listening. I did a lot of raids after that. I volunteered for everything. Anger drove a lot of that for me. I wanted to find something to do. I didn't care after that first battle. It was a relief for me. I didn't feel sad about it, bad about it, I was just really pissed off. The only way you're going to go home is to do this job."

It took two days to drive the Iraqis out of al-Khafji and Shelton's light armored infantry battalion was ordered to cross the border into Kuwait. After the fierce initial fighting and the loss of the eleven Marines, it was a circumspect moment for the unit.

"It was two A.M., February 1991, before we crossed into Kuwait," says Shelton. "We had already burned most of our letters [so they wouldn't fall into enemy hands]. But I kept some and a picture of my son, Tyrone. At dawn when it's supposed to get sunny and you look across the horizon and it's completely black, they [Iraqis] set the oil fields on fire."

To shield their movements as well as to create chaos in the wake of their retreat, Iraqi forces set fire to as many as six hundred oil wells as they began pulling out of Kuwait and back to Iraq. The images of the plumes were so thick they could be seen from space. To Shelton, the orange flames dancing over a vast, flat desert with black smoke turning day into night created an apocalyptic landscape, both bleak and surreal. As his vehicle moved into Kuwait through a pathway cleared of mines, the engine malfunctioned and the vehicle came to a halt.

"I'm watching people go off into the horizon. I get up on top of the vehicle. I took off my flak jacket and my helmet. I wanted to get shot. There were incoming rounds and I just wanted to get hit." But no one obliged him. He put his helmet and body armor back on as his LAV was towed behind the lines to be repaired.

"We weren't engaging in any of the fighting while they were repairing our vehicle. But because of the fires the Iraqis set, it was raining oil. We were covered in it. It was part of our world. It's just pouring on us. It felt like rain, but it was actually oil; you couldn't fight it."

After the LAV was fixed Shelton and his crew headed into Kuwait. "We caught up with company at Kuwaiti Airport and a scud missile lands next to us," says Shelton. "It was earth-shaking, body shaking. Here's the thing that pissed every-one off, not just me: We were supposed to clear and secure Kuwaiti airport. We get to the airport and some Marines raise the American flag at the airport and have the Kuwaitis put up their flag too. It was a photo op and you have to position your-self for a photo op! We go through all this shit and this is what this is all about, to make this good for the camera."

After returning to the U.S. following the war in the Gulf, Shelton remained in the Marines for a full twenty-year career, but while he had job security within the Marine Corps, little else in his life was stable. The loss of the men in his unit and the image of Jenkins's charred body have stayed with him to this day. He started drinking and taking drugs after his return, but he also began an even darker and more destructive relationship that would last the next thirteen years, one that provided some evidence of the secret trauma that began long before he was ever sent to war.

"I started doing it in 1994, cutting myself with knives around the stomach," Shelton says. "You don't want nobody seeing it but it transferred the pain. I used kitchen knives, steak knives, a few times a month. My stomach, arms and legs are pretty scarred up. Some of them needed stitches. The hair on my legs hides some of them, but otherwise they're very noticeable. I wear my pain. I had to put my pain somewhere. It helped to keep me here, the internal pain."

Shelton also took some of his anger and confusion out on his wife. After he shoved her during an argument the Marines sent him to anger management classes. Despite his personal issues he asked for one of the most demanding leadership positions in the corps, drill instructor. Part of the screening process required him to see a psychologist.

"He asked me if I was okay and I said, 'I'm good to go,' but I wouldn't look him in the eye. He knew something was wrong," says Shelton. They approved him anyway.

So while he was preparing others to go to war, he waged another one on himself, drinking and cutting and watching everything slowly unravel. His ten-year marriage fell apart, with his wife taking their three children away, back to her home in New Jersey. When the Marines sent him to Kosovo he was jailed twice for threatening fellow Marines and they shipped him back to the States for a mental health evaluation. He got married a second time, which also ended in divorce. His life and career hung in the balance. He was besieged by both post-traumatic stress from his war experiences and the verbal and sexual abuse he says he suffered as a child at the hands of a female member of his extended family. It's a charge, he says, that his family refuses to believe and has kept Shelton estranged from them for years.

While this shattering of his sense of self may have begun before he ever set foot on the battlefield, his time in the Gulf hindered any ability he might've had left to contain it. Whether from childhood abuse or war, Shelton had lost the thread of his own story, unable to tell it, because he was unable to comprehend it. This is typical, according to psychiatrist Dr. Jonathan Shay. In *Achilles in Vietnam*, Shay wrote, "To encounter radical evil is to make one forever different from the trusting, 'normal' person who wraps the rightness of the social order around himself, snugly like a cloak of safety. When a survivor of prolonged trauma loses all sense of meaningful personal narrative, this may result in contaminated identity."

Shelton's "contaminated identity" was finally recognized by mental health professionals when he was nine months shy of retirement. VA doctors diagnosed him with depression and post-traumatic stress disorder. He was put on a cocktail of antidepressants and other drugs. The only option left, he believed, was to fight for a medical disability retirement package and stay out of trouble until it went through.

Today, more than two decades after his Gulf War experiences, Shelton says he's 90 percent unemployable, living on his meager Marine disability and retirement pay. And because of the allegations of abuse he's made against a member of his family, he remains an outsider, never speaking to them even though they live in the same town. He's given up all of the drugs, prescription and otherwise, but often wanders the streets at night with little to keep him company but his scars and his dog, Rosco. He tries not to think about the war at all.

"I spend a lot of time trying to avoid it," says Shelton. "But the physical feeling, the impact and the sounds of rounds being fired are still there. I stay home. I don't go anywhere. It's in the body, man, it's physical sensations. I don't think no one can ever be prepared, no one can ever be prepared unless you're insane already."

Shelton feels his past has turned him into a hollow man, one without purpose or peace. But he hasn't given up the search to find them both again. He's immersed himself in different veterans' therapy programs in the effort to understand and rewrite his own personal narrative in a way that restores its meaning. One program is called Combat Paper (www.combat paper.org), in which service members make paper out of their shredded uniforms and then use that paper to create drawings, paintings or sculptures. He's also tried his hand at writing, joining a group called Warrior Writers.

This is a piece he published on the Warrior Writers website (www.warriorwriters.org):

I'm a demon in my own life. I'm that darkness that
falls on my own day, eating at my own thoughts.
Destroying my own core. I'm too far for you to reach
your hand out to help me because I've already given
up. I am not what I show you nor what you think.
I am something else. When you close your eyes you
will see me, when you walk alone I am behind you,
when you hear a whisper, you have heard me but I
know you will not find me. What makes you think

you can look for me if you know not what I am? I
hear voices in my head, I hear laughter at me, I know
I have failed in life and I am a tool that has been
molded and slowly spiraling day by day until I am
sucked in that darker place of no return only to suffer
more.

While his observations, like this one, are loaded with pes-
simism and despair, they are at the very least, according to
mental health experts, an effort at sharing the burden of his
experiences and, by doing so, continuing the work of finding a
better, more hopeful ending.

POSTSCRIPT

After the completion of this book, Shelton wrote me
a short letter about getting a chance to spend time with his
children, after not seeing them for years. Despite its brevity,
it seemed to indicate some small glimmer of progress . . . and
maybe even hope: "Hi Kevin, I had my sons for the first time
in over 7 years. I hope you are doing well and I can not thank
you enough for hearing my story. It provided a huge weight off
my shoulders."

The author's father, Navy ensign Edward Sites, left, in Papua New Guinea, 1945

INTERMISSION

THE GREATEST VENERATION
My Father's War

LIKE SO many others in the frequently beatified Greatest Generation, my father never told me about his experiences during World War II.* He served in the South Pacific, a young ensign who ferried Marines on flat-bottomed landing crafts to mop-up operations on the islands at the end of the war. He never told me about his time on a destroyer off the coast of Korea either.

All I knew was that he had been part of the Navy V-12 program started in 1943, designed to do two things: first, to meet the officer needs of a rapidly expanding wartime Navy and Marine Corps, and second, to keep American colleges and universities from collapsing due to dwindling enrollment as

---

* The term "Greatest Generation" was coined by NBC News anchorman and journalist Tom Brokaw in the title of his book *The Greatest Generation*, about the generation that built modern America following the trials of growing up during the Great Depression and World War II.

college-age men were either drafted or volunteered for service. One hundred thousand men selected for the program enrolled in public and private colleges across the country with the federal government paying tuition. They were fast-tracked through three terms over the course of a full year, followed by midshipmen's school for those joining the Navy or boot camp and officer candidate school for men choosing the Marines. Successful graduates were made Navy ensigns or Marine second lieutenants and then sent to fill the gaps overseas. My father was one of them. After completing the program he left his small Great Lakes hometown of Geneva, Ohio, to command sailors in the South Pacific. He was nineteen years old and had barely traveled outside Ohio, let alone the country. I knew he was proud of getting through the V-12 program, which, with its accelerated instruction, put a lot of pressure on its candidates, resulting in a high washout rate. But while he briefly told me about what he had to go through to get into the Navy, he never told me about his experiences once he was in the service as an officer during the war. At the time, I thought it was selfish that someone could be a part of the fabled Greatest Generation but still be unwilling to part with even the smallest anecdote. In retrospect, maybe I just wasn't persistent enough or didn't ask the right questions.

Edward Sites in the South Pacific during World War II

What I did know was what I could discern from the photographs he hung in his den and the ones he kept in boxes in
the attic. They were mostly macho poses, bare chested, flag
waving, not very different than the kind soldiers of today
affect while deployed to Iraq or Afghanistan. But out of all of
them, there is only one that's held my imagination since I first
glimpsed it as a ten-year-old boy. It's a picture (see page 140) of
my father in his khaki uniform, a .45 in his right hand, held
at waist level, pointed in the direction of two rows of Japanese
prisoners with their arms raised above their heads in surrender. I remember, as a boy, seeing the photograph while digging
through my father's things in the attic, but I never quite understood what the image depicted. Though I believe my brother
and I may have asked him indirectly in the years after, we
never got what I considered a real answer. When I went to see
my parents in their retirement community, south of Tucson, a
few months after I had helped create an international contro-
versy by releasing the video I had shot as an embedded journalist of the American Marine executing a wounded, unarmed
insurgent in the mosque in Fallujah, we talked about the incident, and while my parents were empathetic and supportive,
I remember my father casually noting that during his deployment to the Pacific during World War II, they had orders not
to take prisoners. I immediately began to wonder then about
the photograph. It became an object of incongruity for me—
an obsession really. My father, I had always believed, was an
uncompromisingly moral man. As a small-town savings and
loan executive he would return Christmas fruit baskets from

clients, sending a message that he would not be swayed one way or another concerning their loan applications, whether that was their intention or not. But in this case, was my father trying to tell me that in war the same rules of civilized society didn't apply? After all, how can you agree there are going to be rules if you're already killing each other? But deep down this was my fear: Was this man who had seen me through my childhood, the doting and dutiful husband, weekend golfer and George Bailey–type small-town savings and loan officer, also a cold-blooded killer? Could the unarmed prisoners he held at gunpoint have become his victims as well? Could my father have done what so many others had done before, justified a summary execution of those who might've killed him had the roles been reversed? Over the years, I replayed his every dinner-table utterance in my mind: the anger over what the Japanese had done at Pearl Harbor, his robust defense of the dropping of atomic bombs on Hiroshima and Nagasaki. Was there, I wondered, a dark-hearted beast under this mostly kind façade he kept?

Ironically, despite my sense of duty in reporting the truth where the mosque was concerned, I never found the courage to ask him, my own father, if he was capable of acting, or indeed had acted, in the same way as the Marine in Fallujah.

As age took away some of his agility and most of his sight from macular degeneration, I watched my father, a giant of my memories, physically shrink before my eyes. His life was now mostly about comforting my mother, also a veteran, a Navy flight nurse during the Korean War, whose back had been wracked by the abuse of an unforgiving thirty-five-year career as a surgical nurse, and listening to audiobooks provided to him by the VA.

Each time I visited them I pretended it was the time I would ask him, but instead I rationalized that it was better not to kick over that rock. I lived for years with my circumstantial suspicions but never worked up the courage to ask him directly. But that didn't stop my older brother, Tim. One Christmas when we were both visiting, Tim and I had lunch with my father in the dining room of his assisted-living residence. We were talking about the progress of my book when my brother simply blurted out, "Dad, did you ever see some real action or have to shoot and kill anyone in the war?"

I was stunned. Tim, without so much as blinking, asked the question that had haunted me, the question I was uncertain I even wanted answered. My father was silent.

He folded his arms, pausing, then cleared his throat before he spoke. "Well, you've seen the picture, haven't you," he said. Here it comes, I thought, the very moral foundation of my belief system about to crash down around me. He continued. "You know, that one of me and the Japanese," he said, as if he had lifted it from my brain. My brother and I both nodded silently.

I waited for him to confirm my worst fears, that this kind and honest man might be no different from most when it came to war. When ordered, he could pull the trigger and kill an enemy who had made the mistake of trusting his humanity.

"Well," he said, "the war was already over. Japan had surrendered and we were taking them to a prison camp. That's about as close as I got."

"You didn't shoot them?" my brother asked.

"No," my father said, as if it were a silly question, "I didn't shoot anyone." I finished my salad, trying to spear what was left of the lettuce greens on my plate. I couldn't look my father in the eyes, even though he couldn't really see me. I felt thoroughly ashamed that because of my own cowardice, I might've let him go to his grave with his son doubting the character he had never given him cause to doubt. But I knew I was also subtly disappointed that his moral nature had robbed me of a narrative irony too good to be true. But that is perhaps the greatest danger of telling war stories—our desire to make them mean something more than what they are.

POSTSCRIPT

Still ashamed of my wrong assumptions, I'm somewhat relieved that because of his poor vision, my father will likely never read this book.

PART III

Things That Stain the Soul

What Can Never Be Forgotten?

THE WALL WITHIN

There is one other wall, of course.
One we never speak of.
One we never see,
One which separates memory from madness.
In a place no one offers flowers.
THE WALL WITHIN.
We permit no visitors.
Mine looks like any of a million
nameless, brick walls—
it stands in the tear-down ghetto of my soul;
that part of me which reason avoids
for fear of dirtying its clothes
and from atop which my sorrow and my rage
hurl bottles and invectives
at the rolled-up windows
of my passing youth.
Do you know the wall I mean?

—Steve Mason, U.S. Army captain (Vietnam), poet
Excerpted from the poem "The Wall Within" by
Steve Mason, a decorated Vietnam combat veteran
considered the unofficial poet laureate of the Vietnam
War. "The Wall Within" was read at the 1984
dedication of the Vietnam Veterans Memorial in
Washington, DC, and was entered in its entirety into
the Congressional Record.

Specialist Joe Caley, U.S. Army
1st Cavalry, 25th Infantry
The War in Vietnam (1968–70)

CHAPTER 5

||||||||||||||||||||||||||||||||||||||||||||

DOGS OF WAR

I saw their color and the bugs . . .
and then I threw up.

THERE ARE a couple of distinct reactions one experiences the first time one views bodies that have been dispatched with violence. One is a morbid but compelling curiosity to see the things in all their grotesque splendor, to leave nothing to the imagination by savoring the irreparable destruction of human flesh and bone. Another is to glimpse them involuntarily and promptly puke. That was Joe Caley's reaction the first time he went into the field in Vietnam. On his way to join his unit, the twenty-one-year-old private from Canton, Ohio, glanced at the yellowing corpses of two Vietcong fighters bloating in the sun.

"I saw their color and the bugs . . . ," he says, "and then I threw up. That kind of thing stays with you. But that was the job—we had to get a body count. And here were two more for the record."

Caley had been drafted, pulled out of a life that could be defined as normal. He had married his high school sweetheart, was a shoe salesman during the day and took a few classes at Kent State University at night. The problem was that Caley didn't take enough classes. You had to carry twelve credit hours to be considered a full-time student; otherwise you were eligible for the draft. Caley didn't qualify for the student deferment that so many others had used to stay out of the war.

He had gotten married in February and by March he was in the Army.

"It was kind of a shock. I had no intention of being a soldier whatsoever," he tells me during a late-night phone conversation. "But I knew when I was drafted—I believed I knew I was going to Vietnam. If you enlisted you got a choice of what you wanted to do. If you were drafted you were going to Vietnam. At that time, the war and death was the furthest thing from my mind. We were just kids, doing what kids do. Going out partying, etc."

After his basic training at Fort Knox in Kentucky and his advanced infantry training (AIT) at Fort Polk in Louisiana, Caley thought he could put off Vietnam a little longer by volunteering for noncommissioned officer school at Fort Benning in Georgia. But it didn't take long for him to realize this was not a good fit.

"I didn't want to tell people to kill other people. That was an NCO's job. I wanted out, and they put me in Casual Company," he says.

Casual Company was the place the Army put people they didn't know what to do with. It was a holding tank for guys who didn't fit in, whom they considered misfits.

But Caley was presented with an opportunity while in Casual Company and his choice led him directly to the place he had been hoping to avoid.

"They asked if I wanted to walk dogs and I said yes. I didn't realize I'd be walking dogs on point in combat." Caley pauses. "But at least I did have some control."

Or so he thought. Caley's job was to be part of the 25th Infantry Division's Platoon Scout Dogs, soldiers who would handle specially trained German shepherds and walk in advance of other ground troops, an early-warning system, literally sniffing out danger, bombs, booby traps and enemy fighters. In an infantry unit, walking point, being at the tip of an advancing squad, team or platoon, was considered the most dangerous and often lethal spot in the formation. As part of the Scout Dogs, Caley and his fifty-seven-pound shepherd named Baron walked in front of the man on point. Caley learned quickly that if he was going to survive his deployment he would have to learn to trust Baron.

"ONE TIME I WAS telling the dog to search and move and he wouldn't move." Caley tried to nudge him forward, but Baron stayed put. "It just so happens about three or four feet in front of us was a trip wire, a booby trap." Baron had saved his life. "All your faith is put in the animal," Caley says. "When we were walking point we never really lost anyone. I take pride in that."

How Caley and the other dog handlers operated was a simple but dangerous protocol: if the dog alerted him and he saw movement, Caley would raise his M16 and fire. Doing that, however, would usually prompt the rest of the unit to do the same. But being so far out front, Caley and his dog could sometimes end up in the crossfire.

Like anyone going into combat, nerves sometimes got the best of him. The first time Caley actually did fire his rifle in combat, the target was nothing more than a pile of leaves. Caley laughed at himself, explaining how Baron might alert him to something and "the next thing you know you're opening up on trees and leaves and there's nothing there."

Caley grew into the job but never forgot the life he had been yanked from and wondered when he might be allowed to return. His helmet liner became a virtual calendar for his yearlong deployment. On it he had an outline of his home state of Ohio and a pattern of 365 squares—each representing a day. He would mark off every passing day with an "X" until his tour was over and he could go home. While he felt his job was important, Caley, like the other dog handlers, never felt like he belonged to any specific outfit. Since there were only around fifteen dog teams for the whole division, they were constantly shuffled out to different platoons in the field, specialists who were needed and requested the same way you might request a "tunnel rat" or the EOD team (Explosive Ordnance Disposal/bomb squad).* These experts were valued by the units they worked with but never really became a part of them. In the American military, they were nomadic loners, helping to protect and save lives but never really reaping the psychological rewards in terms of band-of-brother-type friendships and unit identity. It became even tougher to deal with when things went wrong.

On one patrol, he and Baron were leading an infantry unit about twenty-five feet off the trail (standard practice since the trails were often mined or booby-trapped) when Baron alerted him to something ahead moving down the trail. From where he was standing, Caley could see the figure wore a white shirt and black pants, but that was all he could make out. He and another soldier raised their M16s and fired. The figure slumped to the ground. Caley and Baron fell back with the rest of the main element while a squad moved up to check it out. When the squad returned they told Caley who had been in his crosshairs. He had killed an old man, a rice bearer. A legitimate target, they figured, since he was prob-

---

* "Tunnel rat" was the nickname for American, Australian and New Zealand troops whose job it was to find and destroy the tunnel systems of Vietcong guerrillas in Vietnam. Once found, they would also have to penetrate them armed with nothing more than a flashlight in one hand and a .45 caliber pistol the other. They were often shorter men so that they could squeeze into the tunnels.

ably bringing food for "Charlie.".* They shook their heads when Caley asked if he was armed. Regardless, he was part of the enemy body count now.

Caley recalls "not thinking about it that much at the moment." There was a job to do and this was just another day, albeit not a very good one. Later, once his tour was over, the rice bearer would return. In describing his postwar state of mind to me Caley stops using the personal pronoun "I" and replaces it with "you," attempting to find distance from the incident even with his language.

"That has an impact on you," he says. "You're human, you're not brought up to do that. That's not what you do. I'm having a tough time with this. It got much worse for me later on. You have a decision and whatever decision you make you're going to have to live with the rest of your life. That was just spur-of-the-moment, you were trained to do that. But after you do it, you have time to think about it and you think about it over and over again. Every decision you make out there, you have to live with the consequences."

He pauses, remembering the deeply polarized society he returned to after his deployment. It was just two months before the May 4, 1970, incident at Kent State University in his home

---

* American troops' nickname for Vietnamese National Liberation Front guerrillas, or Vietcong (VC). In the NATO Phonetic Alphabet (used by the American military for radio communications), the word "Victor" is used for "V" and the word "Charlie" is used for "C," so the "VC" for "Vietcong" became "Victor Charlie," often shortened to just "Charlie."

state of Ohio, when National Guard troops fired sixty-seven rounds in thirteen seconds into a crowd of antiwar protesters, killing four and wounding nine. The environment did not engender rational debate but rather passionate and unyielding positions that often ended, like at Kent State, in the very violence the protesters were assailing. "How do you think it would be if I had tried to tell that story [about the rice bearer] when I got home?" Caley says. "How do you think it would've been received at that time?"

Finally, he adds, "The longer I was in the country [Vietnam], I learned more restraint." While en route to a mission several months after the shooting, the chopper Caley and Baron were riding in was shot down. It landed on its side in a rice paddy. Caley slammed his back against the center console of the aircraft but, like everyone else, got out mostly unharmed. He did, however, lose his rifle during the crash. For the rest of his time in Vietnam, he never sought a replacement.

"They gave me a forty-five but I never went out with a rifle after that. I could work better trying to save lives rather than taking lives," Caley said. But taking that life was not something for which Caley could ever really forgive himself. When he returned home, like so many other veterans of the war in Vietnam, he threw away his medals and his service records, something he would regret later, both because he had nothing to hand down to his children concerning his experiences in Vietnam and because it would make it more difficult to file a claim later for the post-traumatic stress disorder that continues to haunt him. When he returns to Vietnam in his mind, he

relives the crash, the constant enemy shelling of the forward
bases he worked from in Tay Ninh, Quan Loi and An Khe—
but most of all, the memory of the old man whose life he had
taken, dropped in the middle of a dirt path decades ago, while
he carried food, destined for the mouths of Caley's enemy . . .
or not.

Back in the U.S., Caley never talked about his experiences in Vietnam and most of his friends never asked. In
fact, he says, many didn't even realize where he had been
since he saw them last. In the war's aftermath, he took jobs
like the one he had in Vietnam, where he worked alone,
often at night, which was just as well since he couldn't
sleep. He worked at Republic Steel, testing the metal's ten-
sile strength, then as a delivery driver. He says his brain
wouldn't let him go back to school; his mind would wander
and he just couldn't do it.

The war had turned him into a twitchy insomniac; he was
constantly on guard, reacting to loud noises, backfires and the
sound of helicopters. He self-medicated with alcohol and joints
but quit with the birth of his two children. His marriage however, couldn't survive the strain of his isolation.

"I didn't trust anyone and I brought that feeling home,"
he says.

"I felt guilty, basically every time you got into an argument. They couldn't understand why you feel the way you feel.
You just get mad and you can't tell them why. I mean, who are
you going to talk to about it anyway and what are you going
to say?"

Like in Vietnam, Caley felt he had only his dogs to console him. Ironically, it was current wars that finally made Caley confront his own war from the past.

"I saw the soldiers coming back from Iraq and Afghanistan and saw what they were going through. I didn't want them to go through the same thing that I had."

Caley began going to the local veterans hospital seeking treatment for himself and sharing his story with other returning veterans. There is a sense of betrayal, he believes, they all share.

"We have two or three from Afghanistan and Iraq and if you listen to them, they appreciate us and our experiences are pretty much the same as theirs," he says. "Same thing, just a different time zone, a different war. They're getting the shaft from people they were dealing with, just like us."

This idea of being betrayed by politicians and military commanders is a recurring theme in soldiers' stories across wars and generations and is a central tenet of much of classic literature about war, including Homer's epic poem *The Iliad*. Dr. Jonathan Shay pointed out in *Achilles in Vietnam* that the betrayal soldiers feel is directly related to their leadership's putting them in positions that contradict their sense of morality. "When a leader destroys the legitimacy of the army's moral order by betraying 'what's right,' he inflicts manifold injuries on his men. (*The Iliad* is the story of these immediate and devastating consequences.)"

Perhaps because of the sketchy reasons that prompted the American involvement in Vietnam or because many

Americans were drafted like Caley, instead of volunteering, the morality of the war was already in question for those who found themselves in the middle of it. They were experiencing a crisis of conscience before they ever had to pull the trigger.

But for Caley, recognizing this "betrayal" narrative that binds him to other warriors has given him enough comfort to slowly rejoin the society he's been alienated from for decades. Rather than hiding his past, he's confronted it by seeking the help he needs. He's been awarded 50 percent disability and receives about $800 a month from the government. His service also entitles him to medications and the psychological services that he's just now begun to take part in, more than forty years after his war ended.

"I'm probably in a better place now," Caley says. "I understand why I feel this way. When I'm in therapy, when they talk to me they help me to understand, it's not what I did in the war, it's what the war did to me. That was a self-revelation. You still have to live with the consequences. But I'm finding that a little bit easier now."

POSTSCRIPT

In 2010, Caley returned to Vietnam with a veterans' therapy group to confront the ghosts of his past (including the rice bearer). But he conceded after that the process wasn't particularly helpful: "We met with some of the guys we fought against and they said it was just another war to

them. They called it the American War. We also met some
of the guys that were supposedly on our side and they asked
us why we left them. So the whole thing still didn't make
sense one way or the other." Caley said two things have
helped, however; the first was volunteering at a local veterans' center and the other was learning to write poetry as a
way to share what is sometimes too difficult to say. But he
knows that for those who have never been to war, it's still
hard to grasp. "I let my wife read it [his poetry] and she said
it was kind of dark."

First Lieutenant Thomas Saal, U.S.M.C. (center)
3rd Battalion, 5th Marines
The War in Vietnam (1967–68)

CHAPTER 6

||||||||||||||||||||||||||||||||||||||||||||||||

HUNG ON A CROSS

I knew that's where I left my soul . . .
I lost my humanity.
I saw it fly over my head.

HIS PARENTS were both pacifists and at dinnertime Thomas Saal's father talked about how America had no right to be in Vietnam, that innocent people were dying for no reason. So at twenty-one, Saal, without much forethought and no malevolence, did the very thing most likely to crush their spirits—he quit college and joined the Marines.

"I did real well at Parris Island [Marine Corps recruit depot, South Carolina], graduated first or second in platoon," says Saal. "I've always been physically adept and I was a little older, twenty-one when most were eighteen. I was almost like a natural at it. Then I got to Camp Lejeune [Marine Corps base, North Carolina] and applied for officer's school. I went on to OCS [officer candidate school], and graduated at the top of my class, after twenty-five washed out."

In December 1967, Saal was a second lieutenant and a platoon leader in Vietnam, based south of Da Nang. Though he was as green as his uniform, he struck a fearless pose. In one photograph from that time, the wiry, shirtless Saal, flanked by two other soldiers, smiles directly, self-assuredly into the camera, as if there were no place he'd rather be.

When another lieutenant in Saal's company was killed, his men sobbed because they loved him so much, explains Saal. He took over the dead lieutenant's platoon that same night. Over time, he says, the platoon became his own and the unit came together under his leadership. They spent their days thrashing through the jungle looking for their Vietcong and North Vietnamese enemies and their nights buttoned up in their makeshift camps, waiting for them. Once, while on a long-range patrol, they saw a man running across a rice paddy.

"Go ahead, shoot him," Saal said to his men. With three shots his Marines brought the man down. They retrieved the body and, after going through his clothes and belongings, discovered he was a North Vietnamese Army officer. They also found photographs of his wife and children.

"It made me realize we had killed a human being," says Saal.

That realization was not in step with the wartime necessity of dehumanizing the enemy, enabling soldiers to kill in battle without paralyzing regret. To the American soldiers and Marines, the Vietnamese were "slopes" or "gooks," names seeming to denote something more animal than human.* Lieutenant Colonel Dave Grossman addressed that phenomenon in his book *On Killing: The Psychological Cost of Learning to Kill in War and Society.* He wrote, "It's so much easier to kill someone if they look distinctly different from you. If your propaganda machine can convince your soldiers that their opponents are not really humans but are 'inferior forms of life,' then their natural resistance to killing their own species will be reduced. Often the enemy's humanity is denied by referring to him as a Gook, Kraut or Nip."

Killing an enemy in this context was not taking life, but rather stopping a threat, which might save the lives of your brothers in arms. And since the dead enemy wasn't human to those who bought into this belief system, then their bodies could be considered trophies of the kill just like hunted animals, as Saal would soon discover.

"I felt terrible [after the shooting], so I took a short power nap and woke up to see what my men had done to his body. It was fucked," says Saal. What they did to their dead enemy became an image that Saal could never shake for all his days and nights thereafter.

"They got bamboo that was lying around, made a cross and . . . they fucking crucified him. My men crucified the

---

* The use of the derogatory term "gook" dates back to U.S. Marines fighting in the Philippines from 1899 to 1902. It was widely used by American service members during the wars in Korea and Vietnam.

soldier after they stripped him naked. That was my platoon under which I thought I had control."

"Take him down! Take him the fuck down," Saal remembers shouting at them.

"Come on, Lieutenant. They'd do the same thing to us if the situation were reversed," one responded.

"I don't give a good goddamn fuck! We are not them!"

This body hanging from the cross was not just his enemy, not just a "gook" or dangerous animal. He was a human being, a North Vietnamese officer with a wife and child, just doing his job as they were doing. The pictures Saal found on him made that clear. And this triumphalist crucifixion had seemed to strip away his and his men's humanity, not that of this dead soldier, as it was intended. Saal says he felt a profound emptiness, as if he had lost a part of himself forever.

"I knew that's where I left my soul . . . I lost my humanity. I saw it fly over my head. I'm sure there's a lot of souls like mine, flying over the Iwo Jimas and the Gettysburgs." It was a moment in war that Dr. Jonathan Shay characterized in *Achilles in Vietnam* as life-altering bad luck: "Battle creates inexplicable events that soldiers experience as luck," wrote Shay. "These run from astounding good luck to crushing bad luck that taints the very soul."

Saal walked away and sat on the edge of a clearing of elephant grass. As he hung his head, his radioman snapped a picture of him. He says when he saw the photo years later he knew exactly when the moment was. It inspired him to write a poem with these lines:

CRUCIFIXION

Later, depressed, angry, isolated and staring blankly
over the brown, dry and desolate rice paddy
where I had ordered the kill,
I watched my soul, a never regained part of me,
fly with wings, not those of an angel,
but as a dark and sad object,
wondering how this could ever have happened.

Saal explains the actions of his men in this way: "They had been there that entire fall, the war escalated to its peak. A lot of those guys had been through some heavy fighting and after their lieutenant was killed—they had motive for revenge. They were chomping at the bit to kill . . . and to get a body was a rarity. That was a high point for us to bring in the body. He had been NVA [North Vietnamese Army] officer which made us look good."

Saal's platoon command was marked by moments of moral betrayal where an enemy could be crucified and friends turned into enemies. It was the kind of bad luck, so easily roused in war, that did indeed taint the soul. Part of his journey back from the trauma of his wartime experience has included writing poetry to provide context and narrative to what was formerly just memory. He e-mails me a poem that he says was the most difficult one for him to write. This is an excerpt:

NAMELESS WOMAN

I remember seeing you with your long, black hair as if it
 were yesterday.
You were standing there waiting for me the next
 morning.
Waiting for me to enter what was left of your village.
We had split up, paired up, my men and I, and we had
 made friends with your friends.
Had eaten with you the afternoon before, eaten the food
 you had offered.
Shared with you, laughed and joked with you.
Good times, happy times during a war where there was
 little or no trust.
During a war where there were no friends, only enemies.

And then at dusk, we left and prepared an ambush close
 by your village.
It was rumored enemy soldiers were using it as a staging
 area for night patrols.
And the rumor proved true.
At midnight, a patrol came through and tripped our
 ambush.
A firefight ensued, the enemy retreated into your village
 and I did as I was so well-trained to do.
I called for an artillery strike, not once, not twice, but
 three times,
until the shelling stopped and all was quiet again.

Just the smoke and the dust filled the air and the only
    sounds were those of the jungle night.

At daybreak we swept through to see the results
and there you were, there you were, staring at me,
    preventing me from passing.
Standing in front of me with riveting eyes which
    penetrated my heart to the very depths of my soul.
I pretended you weren't there with those glaring eyes
    that I have seen time after time in my dreams,
Night sweats that I have had over and over, so often that
    I've lost count,
Night howls that haunt me as do murdered ghosts
    seeking vengeance.

During his tour, Saal saw some of the most savage fighting of the war, including the January 1968 Tet Offensive, in which eighty thousand North Vietnamese and Vietcong troops staged a coordinated wave of attacks against a hundred cities. Saal himself became a casualty of that fighting, which ended his duty in Vietnam.

One of his friends, another lieutenant named Jack, had been killed the day prior, after stepping on a land mine.

"After Jack died on the twenty-eighth [of February] I didn't care," says Saal. "I was taking some real serious risks. I would walk on point or check places by myself with just my forty-five. We were being watched the entire time."

There had been several battalions of NVA inside the

city of Hue and when they were driven out by other units of Marines, Saal's unit ran into retreating elements on a mountainside and they gave pursuit. "The objective was to get to the top," Saal says, "and sweep down the mountain hoping to trap the NVA battalion against a Marine force coming up from the other side."

Saal remembers pushing hard up the mountain, so hard that his radioman could barely keep up with him. It had been raining all day, and mud stuck to the treads of their boots and the rocks were slippery. When he reached the top, he found it had been cleared of bushes and shrubs. He wanted to get a better vantage point to catch a glimpse of the retreating NVA. Instead, when he reached for a rock outcrop as a handhold to pull himself up, he found himself floating through the air. The impact of his body falling against the rock face slammed him back into real time. One boot had been blown off and he was spurting blood from his hands and feet. He had tripped a notorious "bouncing betty," a type of bounding mine, which, when triggered, launches three to four feet in the air, followed by a secondary blast propelling ball bearings at the individual unlucky enough to have triggered it and anyone in the immediate vicinity. It was left by the retreating NVA to slow down the advancing American troops.

"I remember what a mess it was," Saal says. "I grew up Catholic so I started saying the Act of Contrition, apologizing to my parents, and I remember the corpsman [medic] talking to me as he was trying to bandage me up. 'Lieutenant, you son of a bitch, you're going home.' I tried not to go into shock but I passed out. I woke up in a hospital in Da Nang after being medevac'd out."

Saal spent the next two weeks unable to get out of bed. His injuries were serious and plentiful. He had shrapnel everywhere, but the worst damage was to his legs and feet, where large swaths of muscle were torn away. The fact that the hospital at Da Nang was shelled by the NVA nightly didn't help his healing process. Saal said the mortar fire was often more terrifying than combat, since he couldn't move and all he had for protection was a pillow a nurse gave him to cover up his body during the attacks. He was finally sent to Japan for more intensive surgery, where, he said, his injuries were met with even more insult.

Because of his transport time to Japan his bandages had not been changed for two weeks, and the blood and other fluids glued the gauze fibers into his wounds. He said one sadistic doctor chose to rip them off without giving him an anesthetic or even wetting them first to make them easier to remove.

He later recounted this experience too, in a short essay in his personal diary.

Stop, Stop. Please Stop

Behind the curtain separating the doctor, corpsman and soldier from the forty odd soldiers on the rest of the ward, the doctor states firmly and directly that the bandages have to be cut away from the soldier. In turn, the soldier asks for some Demerol. "Please, can you give me something for the pain? These bandages have been on me for two weeks and I know because of the dried blood that they are glued to my skin. I've gone through this process in DaNang once before and the doctor gave me Demerol and wet the bandages with warm water before taking them off." With no emotion, the doctor replies, "No, I can't do that. I'm in a hurry and this won't take but a few minutes. You'll be all right." With that, the doctor begins pulling the adhesives from the soldier's wounded right arm. "Oh, my God!" cries the soldier, "Then at least wet me down with warm water first!" "I don't have time for that. There are other soldiers on this ward who need help. You are not the only one in my charge." The doctor once again commences tearing at the taped right arm and this time the soldier screams louder. "Please, dear God! Stop, please stop! Goddamn it, please stop!" The corpsman tries to hold him down and this time the doctor pulls the tape from the soldier's left arm. He tries to wrench himself free screaming louder and louder as the doctor pulls the tape from his chest, then begins to move on to the badly mangled and blood encrusted legs which are the receivers of the most damage from the explosion. "You fucker! You gotta stop! I can't take this shit!" "Listen, you're an officer! Now act like one! I expect you to behave in a more professional manner! There are enlisted men on this ward who can hear you! How do you think your screaming and cursing is going to affect their morale? Now stop your swearing and control yourself!" "I'll stop cursing when you give me something for this pain." "Oh, fuck, please stop!" screams the soldier as the doctor tears the tape along with the soldier's skin from the left and then the right leg. "You fucking bastard!" "That'll be enough, lieutenant! Just a little more—one last pull. There, that wasn't so bad, was it?" The soldier is then taken from behind the curtain to his bed amongst the rest of the wounded where he passes out from exhaustion.

After his surgery in Japan, the Marines sent Saal back to the United States for more surgeries and to recuperate. To burn off the eight months he still owed the Marines following his recovery, Saal began teaching at the Marine lieutenants' basic school in September of 1969. He would pick up a class of second lieutenants," he said, "teach them, then watch them get shipped off to Vietnam and die." (Democratic senator Jim Webb was one of his students.)

Despite what he'd gone through, Saal says he remained a staunch supporter of the war effort, so much so that after the Kent State shootings, Saal yelled at his brother, a Guardsman not involved in the shooting, "Why did they only kill four?" Over time, Saal says, his feelings evolved.

"I became totally antiwar," says Saal, "but it was a process."

Saal was discharged from the Marines two weeks after the Kent State shooting and actually became a student there himself. He had horrible nightmares about Vietnam but pushed through it and got a master's degree in English. He threw everything away from his time in the war and resolved to never talk about it. For the next thirty-five years, he never did.

In fact, he pretended like it never happened. He got a job teaching English in his hometown of Akron, got married and eventually had four daughters. But the thoughts and memories of Vietnam never really went away. How could they when he believed that was the place where he lost his soul? Instead Saal just obscured his thoughts of Vietnam in a dense blanket of smoke that went on for decades.

"I was a pothead," says Saal, which might be considered a huge understatement considering that toward the end of his addiction, he was lighting up nearly a pound of weed every month at a cost of $2,000. Ironically, Saal was getting $2,000 a month from the Marines in disability payments, using, in essence, the entire amount in an effort to forget or suppress everything that happened to him while he was in Vietnam. And though pot was his drug of choice, Saal said he would also sometimes binge-drink tequila or vodka on weekends when he needed to. Yet while he was, in his own words, chain-smoking joints up to five minutes before he entered the school during his final year of teaching, Saal was more than just fully functional; he was considered one of the hardest-working, most dedicated teachers at the school. He was active in the teacher's union and graded papers until late into the night. And despite the injuries to his legs and feet, he took up running again, as he had in high school, running ten miles a day and even competing in half marathons. In between, he smoked dope and avoided his family—and his past.

While he refused to think about his own war, Saal became increasingly agitated by the new wars he was reading about and watching on TV, in Afghanistan and Iraq. He says his nervous breakdown began in the summer of 2005 when a large number of Marines from a reserve unit in Ohio were killed during fighting in Iraq. He became further enraged when Marines in Haditha were accused of war crimes and called criminals due to allegations that they had killed civilians in response to an ambush on the unit that left five Marines dead.

"It's Bush and Cheney that were criminals," says Saal, "not these Marines."

By May of 2006, Saal could no longer keep his war hidden in a cloud of pot smoke. He had been feeling more unsteady over the last four years, and America's newest wars ramped up the mix of anger, sadness, emptiness and denial. It overtook him and he voluntarily admitted himself into the psychiatric ward of Akron's Saint Thomas Hospital. On the advice of the hospital's doctors, he retired from teaching and went through the hospital's six-month post-traumatic stress disorder program. It would be his first step in pursuit of the soul he says he lost thirty-six years prior in Vietnam.

"I got in the psych ward and cried for two weeks," says Saal. "I hadn't cried for forty years. But the luckiest thing that happened to me was to have that breakdown. It gave me an opportunity to quit [pot and alcohol]. If that hadn't happened you wouldn't be talking to me now. It was just a matter of turning my steering wheel."

After quitting his addictions and establishing a clear head for the first time in decades, Saal began coming to terms with the war that almost killed him and that he believed had certainly taken his soul.

But his life-changing decisions came with their own consequences. When Saal's post-traumatic stress lid came off, so did the problems in his marriage. Years of neglect couldn't be repaired with apologies. His and his wife separated in 2007.

"I did what addicts do," Saal says. "I ignored her and the girls."

But despite that loss, he still feels his life is getting better, having reckoned with the past.

"I don't want to die anymore and I don't want to go back to the sad angry person I was. When our president chose to send thirty thousand men back to Afghanistan after he said he was going to end it, I didn't let it drive me crazy. I still have nightmares, but they don't bother me as much now that I'm not drinking tequila and smoking pot."

He no longer teaches high school English but now fills his days working at Freedom House, a homeless shelter for war veterans. He also volunteers at the detox and psychiatric wards of Saint Thomas Hospital. He said while some veterans like him finally do break down and ask for help, so many others don't and continue a downward spiral of drug and alcohol abuse as a form of self-medication.

"For every one who comes in, ten don't. For every ten who

come in, eight relapse. The mind starts yapping to you, 'Sobriety isn't very fun, I'm going back down to the bar.' I talk to people every day that relapse."

Saal has been clean six years in May 2012, exactly forty-two years after he was discharged from the Marines.

"You don't come home from war the same way you went," he says. "I'm doing a lot of writing now. I could never write poetry myself until the last three months. Now it comes out like crazy. I'm getting to do this stuff today all because I quit drinking and drugging and turned my life around. I sponsor recovering addicts, giving back. I want to do this work until I die. It works if you live it. I don't wake up wanting to get high. It's primarily because I try to live the program. What else the fuck can I ask for? I still teach, but now I teach veterans and others and, in turn, I continue to teach myself the process of recovery from the effects of trauma."

Thomas Saal's is the kind of bittersweet success story that is common for combat veterans willing to confront the demons of their past. Dr. Jonathan Shay wrote in *Achilles in Vietnam*, "If recovery means return to trusting innocence, recovery is not possible. Recovered survivors of severe trauma adapt their own lives, including their limitations, with passion and existential authority. These veterans can become profoundly valuable human beings, even if their accomplishments in the world are often limited."

Saal also belongs to a support group called Warriors' Journey Home, founded by psychologist Edward Tick, author of *War and the Soul: Healing Our Nation's Veterans from Post-*

Traumatic Stress Disorder. Part of Tick's practice involves bringing Vietnam veterans back to Vietnam to confront the war they left physically so long ago but that has never left their psyche.

In October of 2010, Thomas Saal went back to Vietnam on a trip with Dr. Tick and visited the site of his most traumatic experience: the place where his men crucified the NVA officer. He sent me this e-mail response to my question of whether he was able to find his soul:

> *The trip was absolutely wonderful and yes, I did find*
> *my soul right where I left it 42 years ago . . . I was also*
> *able to read my poetry with North Vietnamese and*
> *Vietcong soldiers . . . In addition, I handed out over 50*
> *Beenie Babies to children of the school which my officer*
> *class built 10 years ago . . . My picture was plastered*
> *all over the front page of Vietnamese newspapers while*
> *I was passing out the dolls to the kids and also for*
> *writing a poem from the point of view of a Vietnamese*
> *child suffering from the effects of Agent Orange . . . In*
> *addition, I attended an AA meeting in freakin' Hanoi*
> *while the city was celebrating it's one-thousandth*
> *anniversary . . . What a trip that was!*

Upon his return from Vietnam, Saal wrote the following poem, which he considers the culmination of the recovery work with which he's been involved. This is an excerpt.

COMING HOME

As the soft breeze of the East Sea blows over this land of
    peaceful people,
as the sun shines down on this land of plenty,
as the moon rises up to lighten the night time shadows,
as our group of pilgrims prepares to leave for home
following a new and wonderful journey of rebirth,
I can only be ever so grateful to those who helped me on
    this path of healing,
this holy and spiritual path which has returned my soul
    to me.

There was a time when I felt as if the world had deserted
    me,
that I had no one on which to lean.
Darkness had enveloped me, surrounded me,
sucking the life from my veins as does a sponge soak
    water.
There was a time when I thought my heart would never
    be at peace,
when nights were sleepless and days were dark,
when death's graveyards were constantly in my thoughts,
when dying children, wives without husbands,
when spirit-lacking, disillusioned soldiers wandered the
    tunnels of my dreams.

But today, I feel this way no longer.

The past is now the past—done, finished,
a part of my life which has been put away
as one does a completed novel.
Today, I can once again breathe the cool, refreshing air
*   of springtime.*
Today, I can reflect on my life and accept myself
as one who has made mistakes and rectified them.
Today, I have found peace of mind.
Today, the grave is open and my soul and I are reunited.

Tom Saal, November 2010

POSTSCRIPT

Today, Saal continues to work at Freedom House in Kent, Ohio, as a case manager for homeless veterans. He is still heavily involved with Warriors' Journey Home and still frequents the psychiatric and detox wards of Saint Thomas Hospital in Akron. He says he no longer goes to bed sad, angry, miserable and depressed and that he certainly doesn't wake up that way. Today, he smiles, laughs and even cries, things he never did in years past. He says he's even happy once in a while, as he believes happiness is like a butterfly, something he heard from a counselor and friend years ago. It comes and lands on one's shoulder from time to time and then flits away. However, today Saal is okay with himself, and that is something he could never have said during that first thirty-five years after his return from Vietnam.

PART IV

Deadly Honest Mistakes

What's It Like to Kill Your Own Men or Civilians?

... all warriors and erstwhile warriors will need to understand that, just like rucksack, ammunition, water and food, guilt and mourning will be among the things they carry. They will shoulder it all for the society they fight for.

—Karl Marlantes, lieutenant, U.S.M.C. (Vietnam), author
From *What It Is Like to Go to War*, Karl Marlantes
(Atlantic Monthly Press, 2011)

Specialist Michael "Casey" Ayala, U.S. Army (left)
1st Battalion, 327th Infantry
The War in Iraq (2006)

CHAPTER 7

||||||||||||||||||||||||||||||||||||||||||||||||||

UNFRIENDLY FIRE

If we had just come across them and the terrorists shot
them up, it might not have affected us so much. But we
were the ones who shot them.

SOUTHWEST OF Baghdad in the cooling dusk of late
November, a blue, Korean-made Bongo truck, commonly used by Iraqis to haul everything from goats to cinder
blocks, was barreling toward Specialist Michael Ayala's four-
Humvee convoy. Though two football fields away, Ayala felt
the vehicle was accelerating with bad intentions. His thoughts
were confirmed when he saw muzzle flashes from the back
of the speeding truck. His body and mind went through the
natural physiological responses to imminent battle. His central nervous system's hardwired "fight or flight" response was
activated: adrenaline was released into his bloodstream, and he
began breathing deeply to provide more oxygen to his body's
vital organs while blood was shunted away from the digestive
tract to the muscles, providing them with the fuel for physi-

cal reaction. Ayala's pupils dilated to give him a broader range of vision, his senses were heightened and his threshold for potential pain increased. This is the point for a civilian where the rational mind subsides and instinct takes over, but Ayala was a trained soldier. While biology could amplify his physical response, he couldn't let fear overtake his mind. The thousands of muscle-memory repetitions of his training had to now give him the confidence to make rational choices even while his body was focused only on survival. He steadied himself and readied his weapon.

Seeing the rifle fire, the Humvees immediately took defensive positions, deploying like hidden bat wings; the two in the front pulled off at forty-five-degree angles to opposite sides of the road. The two in the rear did the same. It was how they trained, it was how they fought, and it was no longer a drill but a unit combat reflex. The forward vehicles prepared for a frontal assault; the back Humvees covered the unit's six. Ayala, sitting in the rear passenger seat of the second Humvee, pushed open the heavy armored door, took cover behind it while aiming his M4 assault rifle at the oncoming truck. The soldier in the turret behind the Browning M2 .50 caliber machine gun did the same, as did the turret gunner in the lead Humvee with his M249 SAW light machine gun.

Ayala braced himself. It had only been a little more than a month since his unit arrived in Iraq, but the nineteen-year-old soldier had already seen plenty of war's unyielding violence. A roadside bomb killed a friend of his from their mutual hometown in East Texas, ripping both his legs off in the blast.

Ayala nearly lost his own life in another incident when a bomb exploded on a rooftop where he was standing.

Now, in this moment, there was more to come. The Bongo was getting closer, with the driver showing no indications of slowing down.

"That's when the fifty-cal gunner on our vehicle opened up on it," says Ayala. The M249 SAW gunner did the same. The windshield on the Bongo exploded into hundreds of shards as the thumb-sized .50 caliber rounds, able to penetrate solid engine blocks, pierced through the glass, followed by a string of 7.62s fired from the SAW, which can unload at a rapid-fire rate of two hundred rounds per minute. The truck careened off the road and slammed into a nearby tree, which might as well have been a brick wall. It was an instant and irreversible stop. Ayala, with a good angle on the Bongo, aimed his M4 and fired a few shots into the smoking vehicle. Keep them contained, he thought to himself. He was feeling good, believing they might have gotten the insurgents who had been dropping mortars and harassing fire into Camp Striker for weeks.

"But then my PL [platoon leader] started yelling, 'Cease fire, cease fire,' after a guy in the bed of the Bongo truck slipped over the side rails and tried to find cover in a ditch," says Ayala.

When the platoon leader moved to take a closer look he called for the medics. Ayala, one of the unit's combat first responders, trained to assist in providing lifesaving medical care in tandem with medics or until they arrive, grabbed his trauma kit and ran toward the carnage. What he saw there haunts his dreams even now, years later.

I first met Michael Ayala in early November 2005, a few weeks before this incident and almost exactly a year after Operation Phantom Fury in Fallujah in 2004, in which I had recorded the mosque shooting. I had returned to Iraq as a part of my Hot Zone project for Yahoo! News and was embedded with soldiers from the 101st Airborne Division out of Camp Striker, a support base for the large Camp Victory complex near the Baghdad airport. Ayala's unit, 3rd Platoon of Alpha Company, had just spent a week combing through the potato and onion fields just south of the airport when Staff Sergeant David Crispen saw something on the ground: a raw potato that someone had been hungry or bored enough to chew on. Crispen also noticed some loose dirt next to the potato that "just didn't look right." They borrowed a shovel from one of the nearby houses and hit metal with the first spadeful of dirt. Along with some belt-fed ammunition, they dug up forty 155 mm artillery shells, all wrapped in plastic to protect them from corrosive sand and moisture.

Artillery shells like the 155 were a favorite of Iraqi insurgents, who usually daisy-chained them together for greater explosive power when building roadside bombs. Ayala and the other soldiers were pumped by their discovery. Roadside bombs caused more deaths and injuries in Iraq than any other insurgent weapon. With a little old-fashioned detective work, they found the cache, and because of it, knew they had saved lives. For me, it was a solid story, frontline grunts following their own instincts and disrupting insurgents without shedding a drop of blood, complete with video of a massive "controlled det," military jargon for blowing up enemy weapons in place.

Ayala and other members of Alpha Company provided security for the two members of the Air Force Explosive Ordnance Disposal unit and watched as the bomb experts removed the pointy tips from the artillery shells, where the detonators .were, then packed the openings like snow cones with handfuls of white C4 plastic explosives.

After plugging their own detonators into the C4, one of the EOD guys took a telescoping metal baton from his belt and threaded it through a spool of det cord, walking until the spool played out, a thousand feet away. Behind a wall the pin was pulled on the fuse, sending an explosive charge down the line toward the cache, which would create the heat and pressure necessary to trigger the C4.

A soldier shouted the warning out loud while another recited it more calmly over the radio.

"Fire in the hole, fire in the hole, fire in the hole."

The field erupted in bright orange and red flames, followed by a thunderous explosion. Clouds of black smoke billowed on the horizon. The finale was the whizzing sounds of small metal pieces raining down on the field around us. There were rebel yells and high fives from the men of the 3rd Platoon as explosives destroyed other explosives, all canceling out each other's killing potential.

Ayala walked up to inspect the blast site. What was left was a crater thirty to thirty-five feet in circumference and at least twenty feet deep. There were no fragments left, no evidence the artillery shells ever existed, but the violent force had exposed a patch of potatoes on the left, onions on the right, and the elephant grass behind the explosion had been mowed flat.

I snapped a photograph of Ayala, doing what he later will call his Captain Morgan pose, one foot resting slightly higher than the other on the crust of the hole. In this picture he's smiling, but not all his days in Iraq have been as good as this one, nor will many of those remaining.

Ayala wanted to be a soldier since he was six after watching American soldiers on TV during the 1991 Gulf War. For the adopted kid from East Texas, the soldiers seemed an unstoppable force, rolling through the desert in their Abramses and Bradleys, wearing the distinctive "chocolate chip" camouflage and striking fear in the hearts of the Iraqi invaders while signaling hope for the Kuwaitis held captive in their own country.

"Even though I was so young I knew I wanted to do what they were doing," Ayala tells me by telephone from his base at Fort Campbell near Clarksville, Tennessee, headquarters of the 101st Airborne Division.

It didn't seem quite so glamorous thirteen years later, when as a U.S. soldier himself, he was blown off a rooftop by an insurgent bomb left inside a water barrel. At the time, Ayala and another soldier were doing overwatch, assuming an elevated position, this time on the roof of a house, and providing covering fire if needed for soldiers on the ground on patrol. When the bomb exploded, his first thought was that they had been mistaken for insurgents and rocketed by their own Apache helicopters.

"I was knocked out for a couple of minutes. My buddy shook me and said we just got hit with an IED. We were covered by rubble and I caught two pieces of shrapnel in the shoulder. I was obviously pissed off for a good while after that." Those who saw what happened were surprised they weren't both killed.

His commander tried to call in a medevac, but Ayala waved him off, thinking the chopper would become a target. Later in the day, his unit captured what they thought were the two insurgents who had placed the bomb in the barrel and manually detonated it from another rooftop across the street. Despite his injuries, Ayala says he didn't take it out on the captives; he was relieved just to able to see their faces, rather than being on the receiving end of their infuriating invisible guerrilla tactics.

"I made them sit down but I wasn't kicking them in the face. I'm sure their zip ties were a little too tight, but I wasn't going to beat them up. I also wasn't going to make them any more comfortable than Geneva Convention required," says Ayala dryly.

While Ayala earned a Purple Heart for the rooftop explosion, it was an incident two weeks earlier that had begun his true initiation into what kind of bloody carnage the insurgents were capable of inflicting on the world's most powerful army.

It was October 31, 2005. Halloween. Ayala's unit had just arrived in Iraq in the middle of the month. The standard procedure was to go on patrols with the unit they would be replacing until they were familiar with their area of operations. This night they'd be on their own for the first time. The mission was a route clearing, to make sure the roads leading into and out of the base were clear of roadside bombs. Three or four miles southwest of Baghdad they found one—or it found them.

"The truck that got hit was second in convoy," Ayala says, recalling the incident. "I was out in front looking for wires and then heard a really loud blast. A cloud of smoke covered everything. I could see the front of our truck, but nothing behind it. I thought the whole convoy had been blown."

Ayala ran into the smoke plume, finding behind it a Hieronymus Bosch–like scene of hellfire, anguish and destruction. As the smoke cleared it revealed mangled, smoldering metal and dead and dying comrades. The men were from Alpha Company, same as Ayala's, but a different platoon. The first man Ayala saw was a private missing a leg at midthigh and had been spurting bright red blood from his femoral artery, a bleeding emergency that could end in death within just four minutes. A medic had already applied a tourniquet, so Ayala began a head-to-toe check for secondary injuries, examining the private for contusions, hidden punctures, broken bones, anything that could further compromise his chances of survival. Ayala had so much adrenaline pumping he thought his hands might have been shaking had he not needed them to help the soldier. While the private seemed stable for the moment, the condition wouldn't last. He would die from internal injuries while waiting to be evacuated.

Nearby, another private, the turret gunner of the Humvee that took the full blast of the roadside bomb, was already dead, and a first sergeant would die of his wounds while in the medevac helicopter heading for a CSH, or combat support hospital. But the casualty that affected Ayala the most is actually someone he knew, a specialist from the same part of East Texas where he grew up. The soldier had both of his legs blown off by the explosion. By the time Ayala reached him, the medic had already sedated the soldier with morphine.

"There wasn't much I could do," says Ayala. "I just held his hand and reassured him we got the birds on the way." The soldier, Ayala would learn later, died from his injuries. Just two weeks into his Iraq tour and Ayala had already had his first combat baptism by blood and fire. He thought that if it had been a firefight it would've been okay, but this was different. They were fighting an enemy who wreaked deadly havoc without being seen. How could you fight someone like that? Ayala didn't sleep that night.

"I just sat in my bunk," he says, replaying the aftermath of the attack. "I thought to myself, It will be a miracle if the rest of us make it out of this [the war] intact. I was worried that it was all going to be like this."

He was anxious and jumpy as the weeks went on, every time he went out on patrol.

"I just had to suck it up and do what I was doing. IEDs and small-arms fire kept me on my toes."

What increased Ayala's anxiety was the fact that aside from the other soldiers in his unit, there were few people he felt he could talk to about what he had already seen in Iraq. Neither his girlfriend nor his brother, a Marine at that time, seemed to understand when he tried to explain what was going on inside his head. And he didn't want to worry his parents by sharing details about how members of his own company were already being killed in the first month of his deployment.

CHRISTINE MCDANIELS WASN'T READY to be a mother. She was young, just seventeen and still in high school. When her son, Michael, was born, she did what she thought was right for everyone involved. She immediately gave him up for adoption. Bob and Pam Ayala were told that it wasn't likely they'd be able to have children of their own, so they were eager to adopt. Michael would be their first. They would eventually adopt four children as well as having one boy of their own. Bob was a successful contemporary Christian music singer/songwriter who had lost his eyesight to retinitis pigmentosa when he was just twenty years old. Despite his handicap, he made a solid living touring churches and revivals around the country and appearing on albums for the rapture-influenced Christian music band Last Days Ministries. Michael Ayala was brought up as an Evangelical Christian, being homeschooled, marching in Christian pro-life rallies with his family and even accompanying his adopted father on guitar during some of the worship services. But since Bob was often on the road, Ayala grew closer to his adopted mother.

When Ayala was fifteen, Bob moved the family from Texas to New Hampshire to take a job as a worship coordinator at Grace Fellowship Church. The young Ayala missed Texas but wasn't going to let the move derail his plans. As a high school junior he joined the New Hampshire National Guard in an early-enlistment program that would allow him to finish school before beginning active duty. As a senior he trained with them. After completing high school in 2004 he went straight to basic training. Ayala knew what he wanted, infantry, but not the mechanized divisions. Tanks and Bradleys weren't his style. He was going airborne. After basic training at Fort Benning in Georgia, he was sent to Fort Campbell in Kentucky to become part of the 101st Airborne Screaming Eagles, renowned for their bravery and high casualty rate during their World War II D-Day parachute drop behind German lines in occupied France. In October 2005, Michael Ayala would be in Iraq with the history-making division.

WHEN AYALA REACHED THE blue Bongo truck he felt sick to his stomach. The front end was lodged in the tree and black engine smoke and white radiator steam mixed in a hissing gas double helix. In a moment of cognitive dissonance, Ayala couldn't believe it was all real. The men they had just shot weren't Iraqi insurgents. They were fellow American soldiers. But how did this happen? It's the thing soldiers dread most in the heat of battle: accidentally killing your own men. In formal military parlance it was called a "blue on blue" incident, or the weirdly ironic "friendly fire," but for those in the middle of it, this kind of situation was also referred to by another commonly used military expression, FUBAR, "fucked up beyond all recognition."

The men they had fired on were now either dead or wounded. The one who had slipped from the Bongo truck trying to escape, a lieutenant and the platoon leader, was lying in a ditch on the side of the road. Three others were still in the bed of the truck, an Iraqi interpreter who had been grazed by a round from Ayala's unit, a radio operator whose left arm had been shredded by another and the unit's own medic, hit in the leg by a ricochet.

"The medic was screaming at us," Ayala says, " 'What the hell were you guys doing,' while still hobbling around trying to treat the other two men even though he was wounded too." But as Ayala approached the door to the truck's cab, the medic's voice became distant in Ayala's mind, almost as if he was shouting from the inside of a thickly insulated room. Ayala's hand reached for the passenger-side door handle and pulled it open. Inside there was blood splattered everywhere, but the two men were still sitting upright in their seats. They were dead, riddled with high-caliber rounds. Despite the fact that their faces had sunk into the indentations in their skulls, Ayala recognized them as two sergeants he'd seen around almost every day back at Camp Striker, Sergeant Adam Crain, the driver, and Staff Sergeant Phillip Nardone (their names have been changed to protect the privacy of their families) in the passenger seat. Despite his shock, Ayala knew there was nothing he could do for the men and he moved on to the survivors he could help. The medic from Ayala's unit was already tending to the lieutenant who had tried to take cover in the ditch. He was the only member of the group who had not been hit by the "friendly fire." He had been shot earlier during an engagement with insurgents, the very fire-fight the men in the speeding blue Bongo truck were trying to flee. He had been struck by a rifle round from an AK-47 that entered above his body armor through his upper left shoulder and exited his back. In the process, it collapsed his lung, a life-threatening emergency if not treated immediately. With plastic and tape, the medic fashioned a rectangular occlusive dressing, sealed over three ends with one side left open. This field dressing keeps outside air from being pulled into the lung cavity by forming an airtight seal when the officer breathes in but also allows air to escape when he exhales. Ayala spiked an IV bag filled with water and saline while the medic inserted a needle in the man's arm.

After treating the lieutenant, Ayala and the medic moved down their triage line, next applying a tourniquet to the arm of the linebacker-sized radio operator whose very bulk may have helped him to survive his wounds. They patched up the medic's leg and finally put a bandage where a bullet had grazed the head of the interpreter. When the soldier who had manned the M249 SAW in Ayala's convoy learned what had happened he began to vomit. The .50 cal gunner wept. Their days of service in these or other wars, no matter how remarkable, no matter how brave or heroic their actions, would now be forever overshadowed by this moment, this honest but irreversible mistake. "If we had just come across them and the terrorists shot them up, it might not have affected us so much. But we were the ones who shot them."

SINCE THEY DIDN'T HAVE any body bags, Ayala and another soldier moved Crain's and Nardone's bodies from the truck cab and covered them with ponchos. To get to Crain's body Ayala had to crawl across the blood-soaked front seat because the driver's-side door was obstructed by the tree. When they moved Nardone, his hand, severed by bullets, fell to the ground. Ayala's platoon leader called in a medevac to move the four wounded men first. Because of a delay with the second medevac, Ayala sat up all night with the two remaining bodies. A sad and eerie feeling came over him as he looked at the dark shapes lying on the stretchers at his feet. When the chopper finally arrived before sunrise the next morning, Ayala and his fellow soldiers pulled on their night-vision goggles so they could see the terrain as they carried the bodies a hundred meters away to the landing zone.

It would be a month before all the testimony was given and the investigation into the incident concluded. Ayala's unit, 3rd Platoon of Alpha Company, was found to have acted appropriately given the circumstances of the incident. But the details of what actually happened to the men in the Bongo truck are like a veritable Rube Goldberg device in which every action led surely but implausibly to the next, culminating in a tragedy of the absurd. It began with the unit's 2nd Platoon going on a foot patrol through a nearby village. One of the teams made contact with insurgents and exchanged fire. Their lieutenant was wounded in the firefight. But because their radio had also been hit, they had no way to call for an evacuation. Staff Sergeant Nardone took charge and commandeered the Iraqi

Bongo truck, loaded in the wounded lieutenant and the rest of his men and headed for friendly lines. Hearing reports of a clash, Ayala's unit was called out as the Quick Reaction Force to provide support to the units under attack. That's when Ayala's convoy and the Bongo truck began their deadly collision course. Nardone's men covered their retreat by firing their M4s from the back of the Bongo truck. When Ayala's unit saw the flashes, they believed they were being fired on and did what they were trained to do when encountering a hostile enemy—destroy them.

Before the report exonerated the soldiers for the "friendly fire" killings, tensions were high between Ayala's 3rd Platoon, responsible for the shootings, and 2nd Platoon, whose members were the casualties in the incident.

"Everyone thought it was our fault. That we got trigger-happy," says Ayala. "But after the report we all kind of breathed a sigh of relief."

But the troubles wouldn't end there. Immediately after the incident, Ayala and other members of his platoon had difficulty getting back to the business of war.

"I was really hesitant to pull the trigger, but luckily we weren't in any 'shoot or you die'–type deals," says Ayala. "I really didn't want to shoot unless I had to. I didn't want to make the same mistake twice."

The trauma of the event invaded Ayala's sleep, giving him picture-for-picture nightmares of what happened, sometimes as often as several times a week. Eventually, the images followed him from the end of his deployment in Iraq all the way back home. In an effort to outrun them, he married his girl-friend, his best friend's little sister, who was just eighteen years old. Ayala was twenty. It was not an easy time for the young couple, as Ayala's very identity had become entwined with the terrible things he had seen and been part of. The memories of the blue-on-blue incident were like vines wrapped around a tree, both squeezing the life out of him and holding him in place, tethering him to that November day in 2005. He avoided crowds, nearly jumped out of his skin during a Fourth of July fireworks display and kept a loaded shotgun leaning against the bed, paranoid someone would break into the house. At night, believing he was still in Iraq, he would sometimes roughly shake his wife awake and tell her it was her turn for guard duty. Other times she would wake him, telling him he was shouting out random phrases in Arabic. His life became a mixed bag of corrective medications. He began taking loraz-epam for depression, Celexa for anxiety, Ambien to sleep. The Ambien led to sleepwalking and episodes where Ayala would turn on all the lights in the house and toss the towels and bed-ding on the floor, almost as if he were searching for weapons in Iraqi homes during his deployment.

Even with all the medications, he would still sometimes wake up covered in sweat and hyperventilating. Despite all the challenges of his return, Ayala's wife became pregnant and gave birth to a baby girl they named Kyleigh. But the happi-ness of having a new daughter couldn't assuage the pressures presented by the couple's youth and Ayala's post-traumatic stress. The marriage ended after just two years. Ayala knew he needed help and the medications weren't working. He wanted to talk to someone about his issues related to his deployment, but still being in the military, he knew that could be a tricky path that could hamstring or end your career by getting you labeled mentally unfit for service. Ayala was willing to take the risk, especially since his burden was compounded by a personal tragedy. His adopted mother, Pam, was diagnosed with cervical cancer. Her condition deteriorated quickly and she died on May 13, 2008, while Ayala was on a plane from Fort Benning in Georgia to New Hampshire, on his way to see her. Now the person he probably trusted most would no longer be there for him.

"A lot of guys don't want to be seen as weak," he says. "But my feeling is, if you need help, you need help."

Ayala found it through an Army Family Life chaplain at Fort Benning who had just been training in EMDR (eye movement desensitization and reprocessing) therapy. The technique induces rapid eye movement in the patient, who follows the therapist's finger or a light bar with their eyes, theoretically opening up a channel of the brain to help the patient to neutralize the negative thoughts or memories that plague them.

"He just kept asking me a series of questions that took me from that place in my mind where I was a screwup to 'I'm a good guy, just bad things happened to me,'" says Ayala. After a series of these sessions he began to improve and eventually stopped taking the antidepressants and sleep aids that had been prescribed for him. He says he still has the occasional nightmare about the friendly-fire incident, especially as the anniversary of the date it happened draws near. But he's in a better place.

While time and therapy gave him some healing and perspective on the harrowing events of his first combat deployment, in the spring of 2010 he was sent to war again, this time to Afghanistan. No longer the innocent child watching Gulf War soldiers on television, he felt as if he'd seen enough war in this lifetime and was not eager to go. Before he left, he wondered how the new memories and trauma of this war would stack against the old. Would there be room for it or would the burden of another year of killing and watching others die once again become too much? He also questioned whether he would actually survive himself. At the very least he felt satisfied that he had done his best to reassemble the jumbled pieces of himself that he was left with after Iraq and was prepared to do the same if he had to once again, after Afghanistan.

"I know what I'm getting into. I've experienced war," he says. "Going to Afghanistan, I'm hoping to get some closure from it, where this time nothing happens—we leave with all the guys and come back with all the guys."

POSTSCRIPT

Ayala sent me an e-mail after he got back from Afghanistan in the spring of 2011.

I got back from Afghanistan about three weeks ago. Definitely not quite what I was expecting. They will stand and fight you much longer and harder than the Iraqis, but they also, for the most part shoot at you from a longer distance. I got promoted to SGT re-enlisted for another five years and I reunited with my ex-wife shortly before I deployed to Afghanistan. It was a struggle over there, I lost some good friends, but all in all, I'm doing ok, despite everything.

An e-mail from Ayala a few months later tells me he's separated from his wife again, but . . . still doing okay.

Captain Zachary Iscol, U.S.M.C.
3rd Battalion, 1st Marines
The War in Iraq (2003—05)

CHAPTER 8

||||||||||||||||||||||||||||||||||||||||||||||||||||||||||||

MAKING IT RIGHT

When you go to war and you come back it doesn't leave you. How can you not think about things differently?

IN AMERICA we are inclined to want to dismiss the achievements of someone we consider to be from a privileged background. We consider what they have accomplished somehow not fully earned, the gifts of wealth and connections likely, we believe, creating the gilded path. But while Zachary Iscol did indeed grow up as the scion of privilege—his father was a successful businessman and wireless communications entrepreneur—the focus of his upbringing revolved around the concept of public service rather than entitlement. His mother had been a public school teacher at one time but had moved into a larger arena working on education issues with the likes of Democratic Party political giants like Hillary Clinton and Al Gore.

Because their house bordered a four-thousand-acre land preserve in Pound Ridge, New York, Iscol grew up exploring and playing in the woods. He dreamed of becoming not a businessman but a marine biologist. But what Iscol did learn from both parents was that privilege was repaid in responsibility, that it was necessary to give back to the community. It was a philosophy reinforced at Iscol's high school, Phillips Exeter Academy in Exeter, New Hampshire, one of America's oldest and most celebrated boarding schools. Exeter's founder, John Phillips, made it clear in the act of incorporation that established the school in 1781 that instilling knowledge alone was not enough; "goodness" also had to be the mission of the institution.

> Above all, it is expected that the attention of
> instructors to the disposition of the minds and
> morals of the youth under their charge will exceed
> every other care; well considering that though
> goodness without knowledge is weak and feeble, yet
> knowledge without goodness is dangerous, and that
> both united form the noblest character, and lay the
> surest foundation of usefulness to mankind.

Iscol took the lesson to heart; he loved being part of a team, working together to achieve something. And although he was on the small side he participated in aggressive team sports like soccer and ice hockey. Later, when he graduated from Exeter and attended Cornell University, he even played in a so-called lightweight or sprint college football league. It was here, through the team's coach Terry Cullen—who had received both a Purple Heart and the nation's third-highest decoration, a Silver Star, as a Marine officer in Vietnam—that Iscol began to think of the military as his way of giving back, as both his parents and his high school had encouraged him to do.

To Iscol, Cullen was more than a coach; he was a living hero, though he no longer looked the part. Bald and bulldog paunchy, Iscol says Cullen never talked about his 1967 tour in Vietnam but carried it with him quite visibly. Once when he removed his shirt in the locker room to shower, Iscol caught a glimpse of three big divots in the ex-Marine and onetime college quarterback's shoulder where he was shot by an antiaircraft gun used to fire on U.S. troops. Cullen took the hits and still kept leading his men in the fight. Cullen told Iscol that if he insisted on joining the military, the Marines were the way to go. He said there was no better leadership training, no better preparation for the real world. While still at Cornell Iscol began a program called the Platoon Leaders Class, in which he went to officer candidate school over two summers before his sophomore and senior years. He was commissioned as a Marine officer in 2001, a year after graduating from Cornell.

"My dad had been in the Air Force for two years and grandparents on both sides of the family served in World War II," says Iscol. "I had a pretty great life; I owed my country something. I felt like I needed to serve. I was idealistic."

Iscol's first deployment with the 1st Battalion, 1st Marines wasn't what he had bargained for. While he had hoped to be part of the main fighting effort near Baghdad or al-Anbar Province, he ended up commanding small boat operations in the Shatt al-Arab waterways in the south near Basra.

"Day and night we were running patrols along the waterway, boarding fishing boats and seizing weapons or intercepting smugglers going into Iran with oil," says Iscol. "Every boat we inspected had signs of smuggling and their bilge tanks were filled with oil. Most boats had fake floors with storage space underneath. We'd use six boats on these patrols; two boats would provide overwatch, with snipers circling the boat you were boarding. Then we would use the others to form a boarding party up," Iscol says. "First we'd stop the boats, asking permission to board. The captain is told to get all of his men out on his deck in one place. Then we'd search for weapons and other contraband."

It was not the kind of action he was expecting to see in Iraq.

"Here were these major historical events going on and I had not been a part of it," says Iscol. "It was the kind of feeling someone from the 'Greatest Generation' might have had being rejected for service in World War II because of flat feet."

But as soon as he got home to the States, Iscol started searching for a way to get back. His platoon sergeant had a friend in another battalion, 3/1 Marines, and after sending e-mails and making phone calls, they both wrangled a transfer to the unit. By June of 2004, Iscol was in Iraq again, after spending only a few months at home. A week into the deployment Iscol was made commander of a Combined Action Platoon of Marines that embedded for the next four months with six platoons of Iraqi National Guard soldiers. Five of the platoons, Iscol says, were made of up of Shias and had a record of fighting effectively alongside Marines. One platoon, however, was dominated by Sunnis and was likely, he says, to have had ties to the insurgency.

It was here Iscol met the most important man of his deployment, his interpreter Khalil Abood. Abood would become Iscol's liaison, guide, teacher and confidant. Their relationship would become so close that some of the Iraqi soldiers started calling Abood "Abu Zachi," or "the father of Zach."

After the U.S.-led invasion of Iraq, Abood was trying to support his family on his $10-a-month pension. He went to Amadiya, where the American Army had just set up an outpost, and got a job working for them. He eventually ended up in al-Anbar Province working with the Marines.

Abood had the gravitas to deal with everyone on their own terms, from poor farmers to distinguished sheiks. In fact, Iscol says Abood's rapport with tribal leaders was so good that Iscol sometimes felt like a little boy trying to be a grown-up when he was with Abood. This frustration came out early on in the deployment when Iscol interrupted Abood during a meeting with tribal elders.

"I appreciate the fact you're talking with them, but do you mind translating so I'm not left out of conversations?" he remembers saying. But in fact, Abood had only been greeting them and making salutations; they hadn't even begun talking business yet. The room went silent. "I knew then," says Iscol, "it was a moment for me to check my arrogance at the door and be humble. Abood knew a lot more about any of this than I did."

"The next six months we were working together every day. He was my eyes, ears and voice," says Iscol. "In terms of trusting him I felt Abood is like Geppetto: he has a very old soul, a decent human being. There was just something about him."

And it would be during one defining moment for Iscol that Abood would provide the greatest guidance and support, for which Iscol would spend much of his time after returning to America attempting to repay him.

"WE GOT A CALL from our battalion that night that a high-value target would be traveling from Fallujah to Baghdad. We needed to set up a checkpoint, put out the wire, put out cones. And since a lot of times insurgents would drive up to checkpoints, shoot at us and run away, I had an idea that we would set up cat claws, remote-control spike strips to pop up and shred their tires as they tried to make their retreat. We set this up on Route Michigan five kilometers east of Fallu-jah.* We're in an ambush position and wait, then at a certain point in the night a dump truck flies by," says Iscol. "It crashes through the first barrier. And our machine gunner opens fire on it"—as Iscol says he ordered the Marine to do under those circumstances. "Then everyone opens up, including the Iraqis [the Iraqi National Guard]. Another problem: we had a poor geometry of fire and some of those rounds being fired at the

---

* In Iraq and other wartime operations the U.S. military typically renames major roadways in terms more recognizable to their troops than the names used locally. MSR Michigan, for Main Supply Route Michigan, and MSR Tampa are examples of roadways renamed during the war in Iraq. They are used consistently across all American military maps and GPS systems so that forces will see and use the same terms of identification during missions.

truck are landing near us since we were waiting by the spike strips. We thought we were being shot at. Finally, the dump truck rolls off the side of the road."

The Marines assumed the truck was a VBIED, American military lingo for "vehicle-borne improvised explosive device."

"We waited for it to explode, but it didn't," says Iscol. "While one of my Marines covered, another opened the door to the vehicle. We saw the old man who had been the driver. He was dead, his dishdash covered with blood. I remember the smell . . . diesel fuel mixed with blood," says Iscol. He's quiet, circumspect, as he goes back to that place in his mind.

"At that point you want it to make sense," he says when he continues. "We wanted to believe we killed a bad guy, rather than a civilian. So I start thinking maybe something else would explain why he ran the checkpoint. We checked his truck. There were tons of white boxes but no contraband. The thing that I remember the most was not the visual; it was the smell. Unrefined diesel fuel and blood seeping from the door. The cabin was just shot to shit. The metal looked like Swiss cheese, all the metal, the bench seat, all shot up. And there was this older Iraqi man, maybe in his sixties. His face was fine, untouched, but his dishdash was soaked in blood." Iscol pauses.

"I felt completely sick to my stomach and nauseous. On one hand you're worried about your Marines and the ones who pulled the trigger. You're hoping to God you find out this guy is an insurgent. Then you start thinking, Could we have done anything differently? Almost immediately I was replaying things in my head. It was a nauseous confusion. You feel sick to your stomach that you've killed this innocent guy, but you're hoping he's a bad guy. And you kind of go back and forth with it."

When Iscol went back to the truck he heard his platoon sergeant yelling at the lance corporal for shooting downrange toward the spot where Iscol had been waiting with the spike strips. It was the same machine gunner who had been the main source of firepower unloaded on the dump truck. Iscol knew that with his plan to capture retreating insurgents, he had devised a bad field of fire. The lance corporal had been right to fire on the truck and had lined up his fire properly. Iscol had just been in the wrong spot. And it seemed clear to him they had also killed the wrong man—a civilian.

"We needed to tell him [the lance corporal] he did the right thing and he needs to do the same thing tomorrow," Iscol says. "And that kills you. You're responsible for your Marines' welfare when you're there, but also for their mental health when they come home." If that lance corporal had hesitated, other Marines or Iraqi soldiers may have died. Still, the truth of and responsibility for what had happened, justified or not, sat uneasily on Iscol's shoulders. He felt very much alone in his command.

"We brought the body back to camp and batted him and took him to the Iraqi police station.* As I was writing the incident report, I remember being nervous about whether

---

* "Bat" is military shorthand for "biometric automated tool," an eye scan the American military uses to check individuals against a database of known insurgents and terrorists.

we were going to get in trouble. I was a little surprised how quickly it was settled. I got an e-mail back with 'case closed.' The shooting was considered justified. When everything was finally in the clear, I worried that we weren't putting enough emphasis on the value of Iraqi life," says Iscol. "We got to protect ourselves but this guy died. I wanted the regiment, the MEF [Marine Expeditionary Force], to acknowledge that this was a human life and that it warranted an investigation."

But the value of that life was not lost on Iscol when the brother of the Iraqi truck driver who had been killed came to the base to meet with him.

"I spent most of the day with this guy and learned about his family," says Iscol. "The brother told me that he [the driver who was killed] married late in life because he had spent most of his time taking care of his mother. He also had two young children." Iscol also found out from the brother the likely reasons why the man they had killed did not stop at the checkpoint. He had poor eyesight and the brakes on the dump truck were bad.

"I called a JAG officer and immediately made a reparation of twenty-five hundred dollars, which was going rate for wrongful death.* I think he [the driver's brother] was scared to death coming to see us. I can only imagine what it's like for

---

* Judge Advocate General (JAG) officers advise their specific commands concerning a broad range of legal issues, but most specifically concerning application of the Uniform Code of Military Justice (UCMJ), which is the primary legal code for internal American military matters.

him. When I'd apologize for what had happened he'd say it's God's will, it was his time. My translators and I were really worried that he would be robbed and killed for the [reparation] money, so Abood drove him home.

"Abood was very deferential and kind to the brother, but also continued to empathize with me. 'It was a tragedy,' he told me, 'because it couldn't happen any other way. Everyone made the best decisions they could with the information they had.'

"At the time, I kept reinforcing that, but I blame myself now," says Iscol. "When I look back on it, I reacted as if there were a fifty percent chance the truck coming at us was a suicide bomber. I wish we had taken more risks. But if something happened to my Marines and they became endangered I would have felt completely opposite. Still, I question, did we make ourselves safer for this action or create more insurgents?"

Later, the incident would also challenge him to think about the bigger picture, the strategic one, about the military's emphasis on "force protection," safeguarding the lives of U.S. troops first, sometimes at the expense of innocent civilian lives, as in this incident.* And after years of robustly defending the mission, volunteering to go to Iraq not once but twice, Iscol also

---

* "Force protection" refers to the measures a military unit takes to ensure the safety of its own troops. When force protection is a military priority, tolerance for risk is usually low. For example, if a vehicle is speeding toward a checkpoint and can't be properly identified, force protection protocol may allow troops to shoot to kill the occupants before positively identifying them as hostile. In this instance, Iscol wonders if less force protection and a willingness to take more risks might've helped identify the driver as a civilian and prevent his death.

began to wonder, after his deployment, whether the American military should've ever gone there in the first place.

But Iscol didn't have a lot of time to contemplate what happened in Iraq while he was in there. As the summer wore on, so did the tensions mounting in Fallujah, and incidents around the camp reinforced his unsettled feelings about his mission so far.

"We had these two puppies, named after our call signs, Beowulf and Cannonball. Beowulf ate fly poison and began convulsing. None of the Marines wanted to put it down," says Iscol. "A Navy corpsman called me over and I put a sandbag over the puppy's head and killed it with my nine-millimeter. That was the moment when I realized this was going to be a lot different than I thought it would be. Thought I'd be killing insurgents and stopping fanatics—instead I killed a puppy."

WHEN ISCOL FIRST RETURNED home from Iraq, he felt a sense of urgency to confirm that his service in Iraq did indeed have purpose. At various engagements he spoke with a zealous assurance that America had been right to go to war in Iraq. But as the months went by, Iscol began to see through his own bluster and did what he was educated to do: contemplate his experiences more deeply. One seminal operation dominated his thoughts, the Battle of Fallujah in November 2004, when American and Iraqi troops took back the city from insurgents, but at a cost of nearly leveling it.

"We came home from that deployment thinking we had accomplished a lot of things. Insurgent activity, especially in al-Anbar Province, was almost nothing," says Iscol. "But when I saw things go to shit again I wondered what we really had accomplished. You begin to see with great clarity what happened in Fallujah. We looked at Blackwater [the killing and burning of the bodies of four American security contractors] as the beginning. But for Iraqis it started a year earlier," says Iscol.

"With the benefit of hindsight, I've become more thoughtful about what we did there. I don't think you can really go to combat and not look back, not reflect. When you go to war and you come back it doesn't leave you. How can you not think about things differently?"

ONE OF THE THINGS Iscol knew he could not leave behind in Iraq was his interpreter Abood. Because of his work with American soldiers and Marines, Abood, his wife and his four daughters became the target of constant threats, which eventually forced them to leave Iraq and take refuge in Jordan, along with thousands of others. At the time the U.S. immigration policy for Iraqis, even those who assisted American forces, was to allow only a trickle to enter the U.S., three thousand per year.

For Iscol, this was not nearly good enough, especially since the man who had helped keep him and his Marines alive in Iraq was now the target of death squads. He began writing letters and making calls, using some of his parents' political connections, even walking the halls of Capitol Hill in his Marine dress blue uniform, knocking on office doors of senators he believed could help. His persistence finally paid off when Iscol was allowed to testify on Capitol Hill on behalf of Abood and other Iraqi interpreters. The day he spoke, Abood and his family were granted refugee status. Six months later they were in New York.

"It's great that happened," Iscol says, "but do we have to hold a hearing every time we try to bring someone here?"

Iscol helped set Abood up in a hotel owned by family friends and then helped him and his daughters get jobs as interpreters. While the impact for Abood was immediate, Iscol's work also helped to pressure the government to increase the number of special immigrant visas for people like Abood, who assist American military or policy efforts abroad and then become targets because of it.

Iscol didn't intend his efforts as a kind of reparation for the shooting of the Iraqi driver by Marines under his command, but it did highlight his determination to prove that an Iraqi life is no less valuable than an American one.

Even so, he wasn't done yet. The young man raised on the exhortations of Exeter Academy's founder John Phillips to combine knowledge with goodness in the service of mankind had more he wanted to give.

"War demands the best and worst of man," he said in an interview with *Fast Company* magazine about his new project, a documentary titled *The Western Front* concerning his experiences in Iraq and echoing its namesake, Erich Maria Remarque's novel *All Quiet on the Western Front*, as well as the questions the book raises about the value and purpose of war. "Fallujah was a very tough fight and I saw and participated in some pretty awful stuff."

Rather than recoiling from his war's memories and his own mistakes, Iscol sought them out aggressively. He wanted to understand his choices and how they might be instructive in the future, both to himself and his country. It was in the pursuit of this documentary that Iscol first came to me. Because of my "notorious" video of the shooting in the mosque, he knew that I had been embedded with another company in his battalion during Operation Phantom Fury. He sent me an e-mail asking to use some of the video I shot in his film. At first I reacted negatively, even harshly, to the request. Early on I had taken a lot of grief from ex-Marines for releasing the mosque video. But then almost invariably, I would get requests from them years later, asking for some of my other battle footage to use in memorial videos or personal highlight reels. I thought Iscol was requesting the same. But he explained his project and then asked to do an interview with me about what I had seen in Fallujah. Although it never made it into the film (it complicated the narrative, which was about Iscol's experiences, not mine), I began to trust that he was really struggling with his choices in war and this was the vehicle in which he could both explore them and perhaps find some closure, by sharing their lessons.

He was attempting to break the destructive grip of some of his wartime experiences by listening to that most important voice. J. Glenn Gray comments on this voice inside of us in *The Warriors: Reflections on Men in Battle*: "Whatever his response, the person who hears the call of conscience is aware of freedom in the form of a choice. He could have performed differently than he did; an act of his might have been different. The whole realm of the potential in human action is opened to him and with it the fateful recognition that he is in charge of his own course. Conscience is thus the first instance in the form of self-consciousness. It is that form that gives to us an unmistakable sense of free individuality and separates for us the domains of the actual and the ideal. Therewith the life of reflection begins, and the inner history of the individual no longer corresponds to his outer fate."

The need to help Abood as well as to produce a documentary about his own mistakes and his shifting belief system were part of Iscol's attempts to extricate himself from that "outer fate."

"I began to wonder if we as a country needed to rethink our reliance on the use of force to keep us safe and why we, as a nation, we had not evolved," Iscol said in the same *Fast Company* interview. "We are fighting two wars that didn't even register as election year issues. Having our troops engaged in combat over there might make us feel safer back home, but are we as a nation simply repeating the same mistakes we made at *that* checkpoint?"

But Iscol is impatient for answers. In the documentary, he travels back to Iraq, no longer as a Marine carrying a weapon, but as a man carrying his conscience. He is looking for more from his time in war than just stories with unsatisfactory endings. He is seeking, simply, perhaps nobly even, to understand.

POSTSCRIPT

Iscol has kept up a breakneck pace since his return from Iraq. He's the founder and CEO of a tech startup company called HirePurpose that uses analytical tools to match transitional job seekers, such as military veterans, with employers. He also serves as executive director of the Headstrong Project, a nonprofit focused on developing cost- and stigma-free mental health care for Iraq and Afghanistan veterans. His documentary, *The Western Front*, screened at the Tribeca Film Festival and is scheduled for release in 2013.

PART V

Moral Ambiguities

How Do You Know What's Right?

War fills our spiritual void. I do not miss war, but I miss
what it brought.

> —Chris Hedges, author, ex–war correspondent
> From *War Is a Force That Gives Us Meaning*,
> Chris Hedges (Public Affairs, 2002)

Colonel Morris Goins, U.S. Army
1st Battalion, 12th Cavalry
The War in Iraq (2006–08)

CHAPTER 9

MORRIS VERSUS MO

There are those that need killing
and those that need helping.

MORRIS GOINS had been home from Iraq for almost nine months. There had been some adjustments, even some counseling sessions, but for the most part he felt like he was doing all right. And then one day he was driving down the road near Fort Hood in Texas and he hit a squirrel with his truck.

"I almost pulled over and called my mother," he says. "It hurt so much to kill something. Or I'm fishing and I hook a bass in the gut and it's bleeding. I feel the same thing, then tell myself, 'It's just a fish, bro.'"

But Goins isn't some hot mess, one roadkill away from a nervous breakdown. He's a highly decorated U.S. Army colonel, ambitious, smart, even managing an enviable balance between work and family, despite long months away on "business."

Some say he's at the top of his game, and there's plenty of evidence to support that. When I first meet him he's in the middle of a prestigious National Security Fellowship at Harvard's Kennedy School. I wonder if he's running for mayor or already has the job, as I watch him work the tables in the lobby area of the Kennedy School, known as the Forum, a popular spot for high-profile socializing in between classes. He smiles, waves, shakes hands and generally carries himself with the energetic jaunt of a successful entrepreneur or celebrity chef.

Still being able to connect with people, as well as his emotions, I realize, is possibly the key to his postwar readjustment.

After a particularly bloody fifteen-month combat deployment to Iraq, he was actually surprised he could feel anything at all. Shutting down was the default mode for so many in the military, silent stoics bearing their burdens in isolation. This was not how Morris Goins operated.

There are twenty-eight dog tags, Goins tells me, hanging from his fireplace mantel. They belonged to the 1st Battalion, 12th Cavalry soldiers killed in action in and around Baqubah, Iraq, under his command. Another two hundred were wounded. When they first arrived in 2006, they were driving around in Humvees without much drama, but when they moved their outpost into an Iraqi police station, it was like the switch was turned on.

"The next ten months were like *Saving Private Ryan* at Omaha Beach," says Goins. Seventeen of his tanks, thirty-four Bradley Fighting Vehicles and thirty-three Humvees were damaged or destroyed during operations.

"I know of only one other battalion that had more KIAs [killed-in-action incidents] than me in the entire campaign,"

Goins says. "We were eating twenty-five IEDs a day. I got choked up during that time and my guys knew it bugged me. I remember one of my soldiers saying, 'Sir, nobody wants to be you, hang in there.'"

And then there was the mother writing to him before they deployed.

"I need you to bring my son back alive."

And another writing him during the deployment.

"I need you to bring my son home. His father is sick."

And during one particularly ugly stretch, the so-called lonely burden of command only got lonelier.

"I lost nine dudes in eleven days," he says.

He wrote all the families personal letters, because the standard letter is BS. "I tell them this is what your son died for, this is what I remember about him."

At Harvard, Goins has the time to ponder those fifteen months and to try to understand who he was in war and how it has changed him.

"I think a lot about the loss of life," he says. Unlike many soldiers both above and below his rank, he knows the value of emotion and not burying it. While still in Iraq, he was starkly candid with Britain's *Guardian* newspaper in 2007, concerning a story about the loss of his men. "Sometimes you can't keep it together," he said. "I don't have the strength. I am human just like you. But these dudes, they need you to be calm and thinking straight, not getting angry and wanting to kick down some doors. That does not mean I won't come back and lock the door and cry by myself. I have eye drops on my desk to clear my eyes. I have my Bible and I do a lot of praying. Then I can go back out again and do what I need to do."

He remembers getting the news of two of the first casualties of his battalion. His sergeant major told him that their engineers hit an IED while out on patrol. He opened his hands to reveal a slip of paper. In it were the names of two soldiers with the letters "KIA" next to them. Goins said he sent a Quick Reaction Force (QRF) to retrieve the bodies. When the force returned, Goins said he went to the gate to meet them. He walked alongside the Bradley carrying the bodies and, touching it, began to weep. He helped remove them from the vehicle to take them into the graves registration building, where men and their body parts are reunited before being choppered out.

Goins called the battalion together and told them "not to forget those guys, send letters to their families, talk amongst yourself, get the emotions out." Goins said he himself was choked up. He asked the chaplain to lead them in prayer, but the chaplain deferred to him, saying, "No, you do it, sir."

Goins said he began the prayer without bothering to hide his grief, tears running down his face, like an old-time Baptist preacher overcome by the spirit. "Comfort the families, Lord, comfort us. Keep us strong and keep us from doing the things we don't want to do."

But there was something tactical about what he was doing and saying as well. He was encouraging his men to vent their emotions in sadness now, so they wouldn't do it in anger later.

"I prayed to the Lord to keep us from turning evil," Goins says, "to keep us from revenge. You can kill people anytime," he says, "a monkey can do that. We have to do it right."

Goins thinks he was able to do it right and keep his men focused on the mission rather than revenge, but personally, he says, it meant coming to terms with the two very different dimensions of himself.

He literally calls them Mo and Morris, reflecting the concept of the shadow self or alter ego discussed in earlier chapters, but for Goins they were simply a way to more effectively explain the firewall he maintained between the soldier and the man.

"Morris is the guy that is out bass fishing and gut-hooks a fish or hits a squirrel and feels bad. Morris is the guy who's really sensitive. But when I'm operational I'm Mo. Mo makes decisions based on fact."

Goins provides me with a simple yet striking example from Iraq of the differences between his alter egos.

"We're on a mission and we're taking fire from a house. Through our scopes we can see the shooter goes back inside. We can also see two little kids inside the house as well. We've got birds [choppers] flying overhead and I give them the order to take it down. *But there are kids in the house!* I thought about those kids for about two seconds. Take it down. Boom! That's not my problem."

Goins is married, even has a son of his own, C.J. He can understand this may sound callous, but Mo's thinking is clear, logical and without emotion. He believes—no, he knows—that he's saving his men's lives.

"I'm responsible for the lives of my guys. I'm not responsible for those kids. Whoever started shooting at us was. Now, I don't have problems living with both [Mo and Morris], but other people do. There are those that need killing and those that need helping," he says, as if stating an obvious fact.

Former Army Ranger Lieutenant Colonel Dave Grossman would likely agree with Goins's rationale. In his book *On Killing*, Grossman observed that properly trained soldiers can become like reflexive weapons, able to kill quite efficiently, after they've predetermined the parameters for doing so. He wrote, "Usually killing in combat is completed in the heat of the moment, and for the modern properly conditioned soldier, killing in such a circumstance is most often completed reflexively, without conscious thought. It is as though a human being is a weapon. Cocking and taking the safety catch off of this weapon is a complex process, but once it is off the actual pulling of the trigger is fast and simple."

In this context, Goins obviously knows his parameters, understanding even before he's in a fight that his responsibility to the safety of his men and his own moral code will dictate when he will keep his safety on and when he will pull the trigger, whether Morris or Mo will be in charge. While those choices can be clear on the battlefield, Goins admits that it's sometimes difficult to keep the man separated from the soldier in the aftermath.

Goins recalls being out in the field during a firefight when two young Iraqi girls were wounded in the crossfire. During the incident Goins pulled up to a residential area where his medic was working on one of the girls.

"But she's so jacked up she doesn't look like she's going to survive," says Goins. Then he heard over the radio that there was another wounded girl a little farther up. He told the medic they needed to leave the first girl behind and see what they could do for the second. When they reached the second girl, they discovered she was badly hurt as well but might survive with advanced medical treatment back at their base. When the medic picked up the girl up to put her in the Humvee, she began to cry and her parents, standing in the doorway of their house, told them not to take her away. The medic ignored them, still holding the girl, until Goins said, "Sit her down—and let's go."

"The parents didn't want her going with us," he says, "so I tell him we can't take her, that's kidnapping. Put her down, we gotta roll." Reluctantly the medic put her down in disbelief. They got back in their Humvee and drove silently back to their base. Once there Goins said he was overcome by the gravity of the decision he made to leave both girls to die. He says that when he saw his brigade commander he couldn't contain his tears.

"I just left two little girls behind," he explained. For the next two hours, Goins said, the brigade commander, Colonel David Sutherland, drove him around in a Humvee, inside the base perimeter, talking him through it.

It was an incident in which "Mo," the trained soldier, had to make the decision, but "Morris," the empathetic man, had to suffer its consequences. Goins knows that while imperfect, this psychological firewall has allowed him to be at peace with himself, both morally and professionally.

Most important, though, he believes it lets him be the officer that his men can respect but also the human being to whom they can relate.

Goins knows that when his year at Harvard is done, he will likely be sent to war again, but this time he will command an entire combat brigade rather than just a battalion.* With each promotion the responsibilities multiply, more lives are at stake and the balance between soldier and man becomes harder to maintain.

"Emotionally I'm ready to deploy, but do I have enough in my well to survive? My body armor is in my garage, it's ready to go," he says. "But your well is not just yours as a commander. Everyone is dipping in it and everyone's runs dry at some point."

But if his well does run dry, he can take comfort in the fact that there will be another Goins to take his place. His son, C.J., is currently a cadet at the United States Military Academy at West Point.

---

* In the U.S. military an army battalion is usually five hundred to six hundred soldiers divided among three to five companies. A brigade is typically made up of three thousand to five thousand soldiers divided among three or more battalions.

POSTSCRIPT

After completing his National Security Fellowship at Harvard, Colonel Morris Goins was made commander of the 4th Brigade Combat Team (Airborne), 25th Infantry Division (Alaska). The brigade deployed to Afghanistan in January 2012 and is operating as Task Force Spartan in a highly dangerous region near the eastern city of Khost and the border with Pakistan.

Major Lior Tailer, Israel Defense Forces
609th Reserve Infantry Unit
The Wars in Lebanon (1989–90 and 2006)

CHAPTER 10

_{||||||||||||||||||||||||||||||||||||||||||}

THE QUIET SOLDIER

*As a five-year-old boy knowing we were being hit directly
by the Syrians, it had quite an effect. I remember my mom
would set out clothing on a small bench in the house so
that the minute there was an air-raid siren, we'd grab the
pile of clothing and run down to the bomb shelter.*

THE CONFLICT is only three weeks old (and will last only a
month) but, at least in Lebanon, it has been spectacularly
destructive. When I meet Major Lior Tailer at a western base
in Galilee in August 2006, the thirty-eight-year-old reservist
already looks war weary. But considering the high operational
tempo of his 609th Reserve Infantry Unit, it's understandable.
It's been mission after mission across the border into Lebanon,
usually at night, seeking out Hezbollah bunkers and trying to
destroy them in advance of a larger Israel invasion force currently being mounted. The unit has reportedly killed sixty
fighters so far and taken ten prisoners without a single loss of
their own. Part of that, Tailer knows, is because of the unit's

experience. Even though reservists like him have left their civilian lives suddenly to put on their IDF (Israel Defense Forces) uniforms again after Emergency Call-Up Order 8, they are not new to Lebanon.* Like Tailer, many of them have fought across the border before, specifically during the 1986–2000 invasion and occupation of south Lebanon.

"It's the same Lebanon, it's the same terrain," he says during my interview with him. "The difference is in the quantity and quality of the weapons we face."

According to Tailer, the most deadly weapons, for the IDF, are the broad range of antitank missiles Hezbollah has acquired, including American-made TOWs, which they buy on the black market.†

"It's complicated," says Tailer, from personal experience. "It's not army versus army warfare. They [Hezbollah] do have an organized fighting doctrine but it's not based on making contact. It's more of guerrilla warfare tactics. They want to draw you into an area where they have booby traps and they can use their antitank missiles."

He believes the only way to find them effectively is to outlast them in a war of nerves.

"The name of the game is patience," says Tailer. "You have

---

* In Israel, Order 8 is issued to call up or activate military reserve units during times of large-scale military action or imminent threats to the nation.

† "TOW" is an acronym for the American-made tube-launched, optically tracked, wire-guided missile.

to be methodical, moving forward slowly, and see who makes the first mistake, then capitalize on it."

For Tailer and other reservists who've suddenly made the shift from citizens to soldiers again, the process is both natural and unsettling. Here at the base, in between operations they sleep, play cards, smoke and talk about their "other" lives.

For most of them, they're lives they just left after getting Order 8.

Reservists call it "flipping the bowl," meaning that you have a nice table set with plates, napkins and bowls of food, then all of a sudden it's turned upside down and the whole thing is a mess, as if the tablecloth has been pulled out from under the setting.

"Emergency Call-Up Order 8, this is a rare animal that is both particular and peculiar to Israeli society," says Tailer. "It's understood they don't use this for superfluous reasons. If you get one, the gravity of it makes the switch for you. It's not an easy moment. It's a defining moment in your life. It will be the difference between everything that came before and everything that came after."

What came before for men like Tailer was history, a complex set of circumstances initiated by prejudice and hatred, leading to a multinational migration here, to this place now called Israel. It's a nation so steeped in conflict and struggle that only the very young or very old are really free of the obligation, when called upon, to kill and die to preserve it. This has also meant that for many in Israel a large portion of their lives will be spent with their identities fused. They are both soldiers and civilians, not either one or the other.

I seek Tailer out again four years after first meeting him on the Lebanese border in 2006 while I'm reporting on the Israel-Hezbollah conflict that will become known in Israel as the Second Lebanon War. A friend who lives in Israel has tracked him down at his home in Haifa for me. I pose these questions about how his past has shaped him both as a civilian and as a soldier. The story he tells is a rich but not completely unique history for many Israelis of Eastern European heritage. He says his father, Yaakov, now eighty-four, is a Holocaust survivor who lost his entire family under the Nazi occupation in Ukraine during World War II.

"My father ended up in a place worse than a concentration camp or work camp. They rounded up all of the Jews and had them walk to villages near the Ukraine border and sealed them in. They couldn't get out so they starved to death or perished from illness.

"My father saw his two siblings [brothers] die on the death march to this place. Later, he buried his father, mother and remaining brother when they succumbed to starvation and illness. The thing that saved him was that before the war he had been sick and hospitalized with typhus [a bacterial infection] . . . During the war, when everyone was dying of it, he was already immune. His childhood illness saved his life but sentenced him to witness the death of his family. He even had to dig his father's grave with his own hands.

"At least when you get to a camp they kill you outright.

At a work camp they work you and give you food," says Tailer. "What they did to them was to round them up and leave them to die. There was no medical attention—nothing." Tailer's father was there for two torturous years—from 1942 to 1944. He escaped to a Ukrainian village after his family died, where he worked on someone's farm in exchange for lodging and food. After the war he came back to his village and found nothing left. He lived in an orphanage in Romania before deciding to migrate to Israel.

He got there after first traveling through much of Europe, finally coming to Israel with the Irgun, or Irgun Zvai Leumi (the National Military Organization), also commonly known by its Hebrew acronym Etzel. The Irgun was a Jewish Zionist paramilitary group that conducted attacks against both Arabs and the British Mandate in Palestine from 1931 to 1948. Israel attempted to absorb the Irgun into the new national army, the IDF, but they initially refused to be assimilated and continued to operate independently.

Tailer's father was on board the *Altalena*, a weapons cargo ship that the Irgun had purchased and was using to bring weapons and supplies into Israel. When the *Altalena* arrived on Israel's shores in June of 1948, the IDF ordered the captain to surrender the ship and its cargo of weapons. When the ship's captain did not submit, the IDF fired an artillery round that struck the *Altalena* and set it on fire. The entire ship and its cargo was in danger of exploding like a giant ammunition dump. The *Altalena*'s captain ordered the hundreds of Irgun fighters to abandon ship.

"He was on board the infamous *Altalena* weapons cargo ship," Tailer says of his father, and when the dust cleared, he set foot on Israeli soil in 1948 with only the underwear he was wearing because he had to jump ship. He, like most of the other Irgun fighters, was finally integrated into the IDF.

"But they made him gain weight first because he was so thin from the war," says Tailer. "He was immediately sent to the front lines. He always joked that if he'd been killed at the time, no one would've known. He didn't have any family left in the world.

"That's why he's a big family man. He loves home; the fridge is always bursting with food. He gets very emotional about things. A picture of a hungry child in Congo can tear him to bits."

Tailer's mother was born in Haifa, Israel, but of a Czechoslovakian father and a Hungarian mother who had both fled Europe in 1933 just ahead of the Nazi rise to power. Their families, who stayed behind, were killed in Auschwitz.

Tailer's parents met at a party in Haifa and married shortly after. He worked for the electric company and she was a teacher. They eventually had three children, two boys and one girl, with Lior in the middle, "the sandwich," he said. But his mother felt the need to help fulfill the Zionist dream of settling the "wild west," which was more challenging than living in a big city like Haifa. So the family moved to Hatzor HaGlilit, a frontier town in northern Israel. The violence surrounding Israel touched Tailer at an early age, most notably during the 1973 Yom Kippur War, when a coalition of Arab forces, led by Egypt and Syria, attacked on Judaism's holiest day, Yom Kippur.

"As a five-year-old boy knowing we were being hit directly by the Syrians, it had quite an effect. I remember my mom would set out clothing on a small bench in the house so that the minute there was an air-raid siren, we'd grab the pile of clothing and run down to the bomb shelter. There was a lot of tension in the shelter because families were together in them. It was the entire neighborhood. There was a lot of solidarity between people but also a lot of tension because of the small, cramped space. We helped each other but also a lot of fights broke out between neighbors and friends."

Tailer says that despite the violence that surrounded him during his childhood, it was filled with the two essentials: learning and play.

"During my years growing up my mother bought every encyclopedia on the market," says Tailer. "We had an entire wall at home that was full of encyclopedias. To me it was more about knowledge for the sake of knowledge, less about specific authors I would follow. I'd read the encyclopedia from cover to cover to garner knowledge. To this day there's still that wall at my parents' home."

Tailer says he was introverted as a child, but not awkwardly so. While he read voraciously, he was also into sports, running, soccer, playing basketball.

"I loved to run and hike and sometimes in the past I would run and play soccer and go hiking all in the same day. I was out of the house a lot."

It was a routine that would later serve him well when he joined the army.

"In the army I was one of the best physically fit guys in my unit and also in the officers' unit," says Tailer.

In 1986, at age eighteen, Tailer was conscripted into the Israel Defense Forces for three years of "regular" service as required by Israeli law. But Tailer was not content to just be another soldier. His older brother had served in the legendary Golani Brigade and he was determined to do the same.* "Golani is one of the three best divisions in the army. It's the unit that won the War of Independence for the country," says Tailer. "Getting there is one thing and staying is another.

"You also have friends in other units and you know in other units it can be better. Easier," he says. "For example, when you go three days without sleep and you're constantly training, you're sleeping standing up. Then you arrive at a tent camp after a long hike, and the officers say, 'It's eight P.M., go shower and then sleep.' In those days, officers could do what they wanted. God help you if you got an officer who was slightly not okay in the head," he says with a laugh. "It's not like that today. So the officer would tell you to sleep. After only a half an hour of sleep, they'd get you up and tell you to put on your uniform and go out again. That's something that can

---

* Also known as the 1st Brigade, the Golani Brigade is one of the most highly decorated in the IDF and is often one of the first units to be sent into military action. However, the unit has been cited for disciplinary problems, including revolts against officers and intimidation and abuse of Palestinians.

absolutely break you. Three days of continuous, grueling training is okay but when you've already showered and slept for half an hour you can lose it having to get up again and go.

"I remember nights out in pouring rain with the entire pack drenched and seeing homes up on hillsides off in the distance. I could see the coil lights of the space heater through the windows and I felt like I was going to break. Another night we slept in tents and it was raining and we were in a stream in a little valley and the tents were swept away with the stream and we were so tired we didn't care. Our officers tried to rouse us and they couldn't. We just wanted a few more minutes of sleep. The tents were gone, we were drenched and had no dry clothes. But we didn't care. They had to punch us to get us up. All of that is absolutely normal [for training]. Some people can take that in stride; others who seem really strong physically, after two nights of that they fall apart. It depends upon the person. Once during live ammo training, someone shot someone else out of sheer exhaustion.

"I took it all very easily," says Tailer. "There wasn't a mission I missed. I was never hurt during training. The only thing that got to me but didn't break me was that I liked to sleep. A few nights like that without sleep would make me crazy. I would lean up against a wall and sleep standing up."

But perhaps because of his mental toughness, even more than his physical stamina, Tailer made it into the unit and volunteered for Raven Golani, the unit's tank-hunter battalion.

"I chose it because that's what interested me at the time.

It had a lot of sex appeal," says Tailer. "We would get to drive around in Jeeps. As a young guy that's cool."

While the training was brutal, Tailer says he didn't try to muscle through it, but succeeded by learning to depend on others.

"You're with those people twenty-four hours a day. I know people in the dark by their shadows. You sleep hugging each other because it's so cold you seek the body warmth. You don't erase those things from your memory. How a person talks or walks in the dark. Say you're walking behind someone for fifty kilometers. you see his back and head and shadow for fifty kilometers, his movements, you remember that, how he runs, if he snores, how he sleeps, what he likes to eat. It's fifteen people you're with in intense, tough situations. You have to trust them, that they'll guard you while you sleep, that you'll help each other during missions. You're intertwined," says Tailer.

But that bond can also be swiftly broken.

"If someone does something that breaks your trust, he's out quickly. There's no second chance in the military world. It's a trust that evolves and is built gradually. Distrust can start with someone not coming to guard duty to relieve the other person on time. Or he didn't save food for someone when he said he would. The team coughs him out. Trust is very, very strong and important in commando units where you know that the only thing to save you in certain situations isn't your weapons, but your people and trust."

Within just two years, Tailer moved from a minor position to chief staff officer of operations, leading men who actually fought in the field. After Israel invaded Lebanon a second time in 1982 (the first was in 1978) in response to the Palestine Liberation Organization (PLO) attack along the northern border, Israel maintained what they called a "security zone" inside southern Lebanon. Tailer served there both as a soldier, in 1987, and as an officer for two years after.

"They [the PLO] were afraid of engagement, but there were a lot of land mines laid down by them. A lot. I was lucky that other units got hit by mines and not me. The first time I remember was when we were a 'fresh' young unit in Yeshiva. We hear over the radio there was an explosion. That they are bringing in wounded. A South Lebanon Army soldier arrives on a stretcher.* He is as good as dead. There are four medics working on him and they know it's over. It's clear he won't make it. They call a chopper to evacuate him and it takes half an hour to get there because we're inside Lebanon. After half an hour I remember"—he laughs—"the pilot radioed in, 'What, he didn't die yet?' As a young soldier, it was the first time I came face-to-face with life and death. It left its mark. For every soldier there's a first time. There are much rougher stories and rougher incidents but every person remembers his

---

* The South Lebanon Army (SLA) was a mostly Christian Lebanese militia allied with Israel during the 1982 invasion of Lebanon. The SLA collapsed after Israel's 2000 withdrawal from southern Lebanon. Many SLA members fled to Israel; others were captured and tried for treason by the Lebanese government.

first time. At that moment I understood it can all end in a fraction of a second. For me it was a big deal. Striking."

Later during his tours of duty, Tailer would have to both kill and see his own soldiers die. But, he says, it was not the killing and dying that would deter him from making the army a career. It was an incident of betrayal with which he was not even involved but that carried a disturbing message for him, undermining the foundation of his identity as a soldier.

On November 25, 1987, a year after Tailer was conscripted into the army, two Palestinian guerrillas launched a daring surprise attack using motorized hang gliders launched from south Lebanon in a nighttime infiltration across the Israeli border. They were armed with AK-47 assault rifles, pistols and hand grenades. One of the gliders landed back inside the Israeli security zone in Lebanon and its pilot was killed by Israeli troops. The other landed near an IDF camp near the northern Israeli city of Kiryat Shmona. There the surviving guerrilla fired on a passing army truck, killing the driver and wounding the passenger, a female soldier, before moving on to the camp itself a few hundred meters away. The sentry reportedly ran away after the guerrilla fired on him, allowing him into the camp, where he sprayed rifle fire and threw grenades into Israeli tents. He killed five and wounded seven before being shot and killed by an Israeli officer who had also been wounded in the attack. It was later determined that an intelligence warning about the Palestinian glider plan had been ignored. But while there was much criticism in the Israeli press about the missteps that allowed the deadly attack to proceed, only the sentry who abandoned his post was charged. While Tailer wasn't at the camp, the aftermath of the incident presented an uncomfortable truth.

"What was going on was the officers were covering their asses. I was an officer at the time, albeit a low-ranking one, and I felt that at some point during the investigation they had lost their direction. It was about ass covering and I didn't feel comfortable with that," Tailer says. "I felt that if something happened to me, nobody would back me. There was no backup. I was good at what I did but after that I decided not to continue with a military career."

Tailer was released from regular service in August 1990 and began his new life as a civilian, at peace with his choice.

"The average Israeli goes into the army at eighteen. He goes from one framework to another, school system to army. You're yearning for the freedom after that," says Tailer. "That's why so many go off to India and South America for extended trips after the army. They want to wake up in the morning, smoke pot, do nothing all day, have no plan. It's the antithesis of what they've just been through. Everyone talks about what they'll do towards the end of the army, where they'll travel and what they'll do. So looking forward to the travels means it's very rare to feel a letdown once you leave."

Anecdotal evidence seems to support Tailer's assumption.

"Among Israelis I have heard a widely circulated belief that Israel has escaped the worst effects of post-combat wildness by sending its young veterans abroad for novelty and adventure before they settle down as sober civilians upon their return," wrote Dr. Jonathan Shay in his book *Odysseus in America: Combat Trauma and the Trials of Homecoming.*

Tailer enrolled at the University of Haifa and received a bachelor's degree in the history of the Middle East and got married just three years after leaving the army. He first met his wife in secondary school, but they went to their separate army units after graduation. Fortunately she was stationed near Tailer's parents' house in the north. He saw her once on weekend leave from his post and they were a couple from then on. They married at age twenty-five. Both were still students living with her parents, going to school, working odd jobs, eventually buying their own place. Their first daughter was born only a year later.

Tailer began his career selling cars, appliances and electronics, but was hired by multinational consumer product giant Unilever in 1995 and is still with them today. He and his wife now have three children, two daughters, seventeen and fourteen, and a six-year-old son whom Tailer dotes on, calling him the "jewel of his crown."

Like his father, he finds refuge within his family, which makes it difficult for the one month every year that he has to put on his uniform and report for reservist duty, required of most Isracli males until the age of forty-three to forty-five.

"It's tough to put on a uniform and leave your civilian life behind. Making the switch in terms of career always hurts something. If you're a student it takes a toll, same with career and same with family," says Tailer. "It's a very socio-matic [automatic] part of life here. You leave everything and go off to reserves. Your son or daughter is sick and my wife needs to handle the kids and house and joint issues together and I'm off in reserve duty. It's not easy."

And what's just as difficult as leaving family, says Tailer, is the reception reservists often get from the IDF regulars and career officers.

"It's not enough that you come and do the service, but then you're not appreciated and sometimes you're even treated badly. You come from the civilian mode of approaching things logically and you've built up a certain level of maturity and knowledge. We work in civilian companies where calculations are based upon education and knowledge. As you get older you start asking, 'Why?' At eighteen you don't do that. Later you ask, 'Why do I have to?' As you get older you get reserve soldiers who are CEOs of companies who don't necessarily accept everything as de facto. It's not easy."

This conflict underscores the fused-identity issues reservists like Tailer face that regular IDF soldiers do not. Tailer must live in both worlds, civilian and military, simultaneously. What happens when both his family and his fellow soldiers need him? For whom does his loyalty come first?

That test came in 2006 with Emergency Call-Up Order 8. Tailer was asked to lead his men across the border into Lebanon to confront Hezbollah once again. According to Tailer, an Order 8 usually happens in three stages: First is monitoring the chain of events, usually an escalation in violence that might necessitate calling up the reserves. He says this is usually a frustrating period where you track news events and try to figure out if and when you'll go into battle. Second is the call-up. It's usually done by telephone and it requires changing your mind-set almost immediately, ripping you from your family and civilian orbit to focus on your duty as a citizen soldier. Finally, during the third phase your orders are cut and you become focused on your mission and the health and well-being of the soldiers.

"My gear is in one kit. When I have to leave the house, everything's already set aside in the shed, not in the house. I have my kids' pictures in my wallet, but I don't have any sort of ceremony or ritual. If it's once a year, no problem. Hugs, kisses and such are the norm if it's normal reserves. But when it's war, that's different. I can't say it happens each time I go, but when there's war it's different and feels different. My wife cries. The kids are tense and ask questions—'When will you come back, can you call, where are you going?' They walk me outside. It's very hard for me. The last one, 2006, was really hard. You're not young anymore. You have a bigger responsibility at that stage to family."

Tailer is reflective about what is at stake when he actually goes to war as a reservist.

"When I came to reserve duty at age thirty-five, I was much more frightened than at a younger age. I knew the meaning of things. When I was young it wasn't a factor, fear wasn't an issue. We wanted to fight with the enemy at a younger age. There was fear, but it was pushed aside, even though we knew it could get us at any time. When you have a lot more to lose, children or family, there's much more fear. In youth I pushed it aside, the thoughts and feelings. The fear came in as a factor at an older age. Doing what I did at eighteen would frighten me to death today."

Tailer may be a keen example of the mature Israeli reservist, a "quiet soldier" who does his duty but walls off the memories, emotions and details from his family, keeping them separate so that one may not taint the other.

"I do not share with my wife and children my experiences of war. My wife hears about my military character, especially in meetings with team members. But in my opinion there is no need to share those same experiences. They have no effect on the establishment of our family unit," he says, matter-of-fact.

"Yes, it's a part of me. But I'm not someone who chatters. I don't talk. I don't know why but it's just the way it is. Some people talk about it and pick it apart and analyze. It's not something I feel I need to share, not at work, not with my son. If he asks I'll tell him but I don't feel a need to tell him. I don't feel it will help him with developing his character. He'll experience his own life stories alone. We do talk about it with the unit. That's where it all comes out. It's not holding back from my family or not sharing. When you're in a team you build a body that is very closed. The togetherness is tight and a lot of things stay inside. There's a lot of knowledge and experience that we share that you can only talk about and go over with a person who was there," he says.

"If I have to sit here and explain to you about this and that in Lebanon, a story of one minute will go to three hours. I have to explain what happened, what the staff relations were between this one and that one. In the battalion it's a given," Tailer says, becoming more animated, his pace quickening as he talks about his unit, obviously feeling the excitement and camaraderie again by just mentioning it.

"It's understood. It's easier to open it up with those who experienced it with me and who know the facts. Lots of times when people on the side listen to our conversations, it's the first time they've heard those kinds of stories.

"I carry with me a lot of incidents. However, despite the scenes that go with me, and I remember them well, they have no traumatic influence for me. Like I said before, I'm the son of a Holocaust survivor who saw his father and mother and two brothers murdered before his eyes. The repression mechanism, that probably works better for me than for others. I don't have trauma that I can't live with or that I can't suppress. I always look forward. I'm less interested in the past. I don't live on good or bad memories. I'm interested in the future and not the past."

DESPITE THE MOUNTING EVIDENCE that combat veterans may benefit from sharing their stories, rather than staying silent, Tailer's "repress it" mind-set is more typical than we may think and not necessarily a pathway to future problems, according to retired U.S. Army lieutenant colonel Dave Grossman. In his book *On Combat*, his follow up to *On Killing*, Grossman argues that soldiers like Tailer, from well-disciplined armies, regardless of nationality, are not likely to become time bombs of PTSD and are often the very antithesis of the postwar narrative we expect them to fulfill.

"They're neither victims nor villains, neither macho man

nor pity party," said Grossman during an interview with me. "The vast majority do not suffer post-traumatic stress. We don't have to undo the conditioning to kill [when soldiers return home]. It's discipline that keeps the returning veteran from destroying their own societies. We also have to find balance in telling the story of the returning warrior, don't attack them like post-Vietnam but don't turn them into victims either."

But Tailer's post-conflict stoicism may be based on a different and more unique model, that of a people descended from a history of genocide, and it may render a different outcome for him as well.

"My father, for example," says Tailer, "lost everything he had and buried his entire family. A person can go nuts from a single incident like I described of his background, but my father kept on living. I don't think that what I did in the army, with all the trauma, was more than what my father experienced. There's no comparison. Everybody deals with what he's got. Good or bad. I look at it less from emotion, although I get more emotional hearing other people's stories than my own, like my father breaking down over seeing a starving child but not over his own starvation. You push things away because you have to and you disconnect from the emotion and work from your intellect. Maybe it's genetic. If my father could deal with his situation, I can deal with mine."

And even though his father's experience highlights for him the necessity of Israel's existence as a Jewish homeland, Tailer says it also has been a lesson in fairness and tolerance for him.

He does not hold his father's history as an excuse to hate or punish Arabs, even those who are fighting against him.

"I get crazy if I see someone mistreating another person. It doesn't matter if it's an Arab or not," says Tailer. "It drives me crazy because of knowing what my father was subjected to. I was very clear with my soldiers: no violence or raising a hand to anyone and honor the other person. There was no veering from procedure among my staff or my soldiers. They knew I would lose my cool if that happened. I was very cut-and-dried on that issue. No wild west. We do what we have to do, go in and get out. The border can be messy and things can get violent but if you don't need to be violent for the mission, that's where the boundary lies. I don't tie in the Palestinian history to my father's. Their story is about nationalism and independence and not about genocide or murdering a nation. There's no connection between the two histories whatsoever," he says.

While he and his father were closer to the political right during their younger years, they've moderated and both agree that a two-state solution, one Jewish, one Arab, is the only chance for peaceful cohabitation in the region.

"After I went into the army I never feared Arabs, and that's not from a macho place. I understood with time the differences in mentalities the two sides have. I don't fear them," says Tailer. "I have a lot of Arab friends. I'm not afraid. I don't hate. I'm not willing to put myself into the realm of hatred. I'm not willing to hate them because that's the lowest form of emotion I could have. It's not a logical feeling, it comes from emotion, and I'm not willing to conduct my affairs from an emotional place. I had no Arab friends during my childhood. The concept of the Palestinian problem formulated after the military service when I realized that to be right about this country isn't enough. I defined it out of my world of values: to continue to maintain a Jewish state with a Jewish majority state to protect us, we must turn into a two-state solution. I must say that I have concluded that not from the Palestinian distress that surely exists, but mainly the emerging reality of an ongoing conflict unbridgeable between the two [Palestinians and Israelis]."

With his last fight four years behind him, Tailer is and has been back where he prefers to be, in the realm of his family. While he may get excited talking with members of his unit, remembering the stories of their past exploits, this is where he lives, in the civilian world, working, taking care of his family, taking long runs with his dogs, dozens of kilometers, alone with his thoughts. While Tailer says he prefers to look forward, it is his family's history and his own memories that have informed him of his duty, his sense of belonging and of who he is and where he should be.

"I also have the feeling that this is the only country for the Jews . . . I know what can happen to us without a country. I know it's very important for us to stay here and see our future and children's futures here. And that's not from a place of idealism. It's because I know what could be. I see it through my father's history. Living somewhere else is not an option for me."

Even if that requires that he continue to live fused, both soldier and civilian, waiting for the next call-up. Or that years from now, if the conflicts are not resolved, his son may also have to do the same.

Corporal Sebastiaan Schoonhoven, Royal Netherlands Army
11th Air Mobile Brigade
The Wars in Iraq and Afghanistan (2004 and 2006)

||||||||||||||||||||||||||||||||||||||||||||||||

CHAPTER 11

INTO THE DEEP

All of us soldiers know what it's like to kill, but it's easier to
talk to people that have been there. Most people don't know
what happened over there. I like that not everyone knows.
I'm here for my rest. I'm trying to forget it.

AT A dive spot called Karpata on the island of Bonaire,
there's an old anchor in about thirty feet of water embedded in the rock and coral that some believe was a ship's last
effort to steady itself in an unyielding storm but that eventually
snapped under the strain of wind and waves.

If you follow the chain from the anchor's eye over the reef's
ledge it will lead, like an earnest promise, into the secrets of
the deep. On this day, the waves are choppy as we make our
surface swim to the spot above where we know the anchor to
be. We give each other the signal to descend, thumbs pointed
down, and then drop beneath the surface like pebbles sinking
in a pond. There's a small pressure against our chests as we
displace the increasingly colder and darker water around us.

We are slightly flared, like free-falling skydivers, but the only air we can feel is in the high-pressure cylinders strapped to our backs and the nitrox bottles clipped beneath us on the D-rings of our web harnesses, which, with 32 percent concentration of oxygen, will be toxic at the depth we're going to but life-sustaining in the shallows of our decompression time, once—if—we make it back up.

For my friend and me, fellow dive master and former sniper in the Dutch army Sebastiaan Schoonhoven, this is not just a foolish endeavor but nearly an idiotic one, yet we feel compelled to do it anyway, to test our courage, to test our limits, to flout the laws of physics and physiology, lab mice in control of our own destiny, trying to learn how far, how deep, you must go to finally forget.

SCHOONHOVEN IS THE FIRST person I meet when I arrive one early May morning in 2009 at the Bonaire dive shop where he is already a dive master and where I will be training to become one.

"Can I help you?" he asks me warily as I walk around the open foyer area, before the other employees get there. He and I each came to this rocky, scrubby little island in the Dutch Antilles under different circumstances but for similar reasons: we are seeking some closure to the wars that still haunt us.

As a sniper, or, as the Dutch say, a long-distance shooter, with the Netherlands army's 11th Air Mobile Brigade, he was deployed to both Iraq and Afghanistan. But he's happy to draw the distinctions between us. Within minutes of learning about our common conflict zones he tells me, without a whiff of irony, "I hate journalists."

"Get in line," I tell him. It's not like I haven't heard the sentiment before.

Over the next few weeks I only see Schoonhoven sporadically, as he's the shop's primary boat driver and dive master, while I, as a forty-six-year-old man, begin my Karate Kid–type diving apprenticeship, in which I paint, fill air cylinders, haul empty tanks, repair scuba gear, fix boat docks and even serve rum punch for Monday-night appreciation mixers with the customers, all in exchange for the knowledge and training I need to become a dive master myself.

For me, as I mentioned earlier, it's a useful and voluntary exile from my Los Angeles home, following the slow, whimpering death of my last relationship, and an attempt to outrun my growing sense of self-hatred stemming from the mistakes I feel I made as a combat correspondent.

Schoonhoven's circumstances are similar only in the sense of needing an urgent escape from bad judgments. Following his deployments to Iraq and Afghanistan, Schoonhoven became increasingly restless.

"I needed to drink and drink, one beer after another," he tells me one day while we're filling tanks together at the shop, "just so I could fall asleep." I'm thoroughly familiar with the process. Insomnia and alcohol and drug abuse are the holy trinity of post-traumatic stress disorder.

Later, after he begins to trust me more, Schoonhoven tells

me over a few beers after work at a bar called Cities that back in Holland he had started drinking more heavily, using recreational drugs and getting into fights.

"It's exciting," he says after taking a sip of his beer and looking out over the water, almost nostalgic. "You're all pumped up and hitting each other but don't really feel anything because of the drinking and other things."

But Schoonhoven knew he couldn't continue this way for long. Since he was also newly married, he had to be concerned with more than just himself. When his wife, Carolien, a schoolteacher, was offered a job teaching in Bonaire, the couple thought that leaving Holland might be a good way to give them both a fresh start. She would teach, he would drive a boat and lead divers underwater and both of them hoped they could leave the wars behind.

IT TAKES NEARLY TWO months of our working the shop together, but Schoonhoven finally decides he trusts me enough to tell me about his experiences in Iraq and Afghanistan. In that time we've become drawn to each other in the way of those who share an uncommon experience. It's a tentative friendship at first, between an ex-soldier and a journalist, but the bonds are forged in a number of ways: through the small talk we make while delivering air tanks to other locations in the shop's pickup truck, through fixing and repairing things together, but perhaps more so when he shares the bounty of his natural abilities, giving me tips for finding the boat underwater before

I lead my first dive and also teaching me how to drive and dock the boat without pulling up short or smashing into the pilings. We've also discovered that we share a mutual interest in the kind of diving that will eventually cause both of us a lot of grief—going deep.

We share a need for danger, like so many in the aftermath of combat, as psychiatrist Jonathan Shay noted in *Odysseus in America*: "Prolonged combat leaves some veterans with the need to live on the edge, to pose the same question to the cosmos over and over again: yes or no?"

SCHOOL WAS NEVER AN easy fit for Schoonhoven. Intelligent but dyslexic, he had a hard time with the standard book-work curriculum. His parents divorced when he was three, creating for him some lingering anxiety and restlessness. At times, he could be a troublemaker at school, getting caught smoking and fighting one too many times and finally kicked out at the age of sixteen. It was, his mother figured, a good time for him to live with his father. Perhaps time with an adult male role model might help him straighten out. The move seemed to work. Schoonhoven went to culinary school and became a chef. Food wasn't about reading and studying. It was real and in front of him, something he could manipulate with his hands, at which he had always been skilled. After graduating, he got a job at a top restaurant in the city of Eindhoven, where he worked for three years. He did well and made money, but as often happened with him, he became bored and restless again. Then he decided there was one job that might be able to keep his interest: becoming a soldier in the Royal Netherlands Army.

He joined in January of 2003 on the buildup to the American-led invasion of Iraq, which would begin later that spring. It was a war the Dutch government would support with words and troops. After completing a fitness test with high scores, he was given a choice of units. He chose the most frequently deployed in the Dutch army, Air Mobile, with their distinctive red berets. He was trained to fire Dragon antitank missiles and by March 2004 was deployed with his unit near the village of al-Khidr in southern Iraq. It was a relatively short deployment of only four and a half months. But while guarding a bridge one day, two men on a scooter drove by and lobbed a couple of hand grenades at the Dutch soldiers. The explosion killed a Dutch sergeant. He was an experienced soldier who Schoonhoven says helped him with his training and whom he often looked up to as a role model.

"I was fucking angry after the attack," Schoonhoven tells me over beers at Shoreside Restaurant in Bonaire's capital of Kralendijk. "All we did later was sit on the base after." With no retaliation for the grenade attack, Schoonhoven says he became more and more frustrated. But the unit never got their chance to hit back before being rotated home to the Netherlands.

Despite his anger at what had happened in Iraq, Schoonhoven was discovering something else about himself in the army—he fit in.

"For one of the first times in my life, I felt like I belonged," says Schoonhoven. "Dyslexia, all the other stuff, didn't matter anymore. I was in charge."

But that didn't mean he stopped getting in trouble. Back in Holland, Schoonhoven's anger simmered. In the barracks he would listen to Nirvana with his fellow soldiers, go out drinking and get into fights. After getting arrested during one of the fights, Schoonhoven knew he had to straighten up or risk losing the only place that really felt like home to him, the army. After being back from Iraq for almost two years, he decided to focus on soldiering. He tested so well on the shooting range that they offered him a chance at long-distance shooter school. He jumped at it. During the training he learned camouflage, stalking and the Zen of breathing, but most of all he learned patience, something that didn't come easy for the then twenty-three-year-old. This carried over to the other parts of his life as well, allowing him to deepen his relationship with Carolien, the girlfriend who would shortly become his wife.

In July 2006, with his newly acquired sniper training, Schoonhoven and his 11th Air Mobile Brigade headed to war again, but this time to Afghanistan.

"When I left this time, I knew something was going to happen," Schoonhoven says. "I told Carolien, 'This time we're going to fight.'"

The Dutch deployment to Afghanistan in 2006 was concentrated in Uruzgan Province, north of the restive cities of Helmand and Kandahar, former Taliban strongholds and still rife with sympathizers.

The fifteen hundred Netherlands troops were the seventh-largest contingent of the NATO-led multinational force in Afghanistan and had a mission statement that put as great an emphasis on building community as providing security. But Schoonhoven hoped this deployment would turn out different than in Iraq; there he had felt powerless, almost locked down on base, after the killing of their sergeant. While he didn't go to Afghanistan looking for revenge, he was prepared to fight. It wouldn't be long before he got his chance.

At Café Buenos Aires in Kralendijk, Schoonhoven grabs my notebook and begins drawing out what happened. He reiterates that he's better with his hands than with words, but that's been obvious, as he's never stopped talking with them since I first met him. He's entertained people with sleight-of-hand magic tricks and proved himself a handyman, skilled boat captain and dive master, and in the past a successful chef and sniper. He believes in the spatial rather than the verbal to get his points across. He does it again now, as he draws on the paper in front of me.

He takes my pen and, as if he were outlining the beginning of my last name, makes a giant "S" on the pad. "This is the road," he says, setting up the story. Schoonhoven says his unit got a call in the early evening that the Afghan National Army (ANA) base nearby was under attack by the Taliban and in danger of being overrun. By the time the Dutch Air Mobile unit could get fully geared up and on the road, the Taliban had made a tactical retreat to nearby mountains. The ANA unit was still at their roadside post, a checkpoint called Chutu, also the access way to Forward Operating Base Hadrian, where the

Dutch contingent was stationed. Schoonhoven tells the story in his own words and hands.

"The Taliban had retreated into the mountains, but we knew they were still watching us because we could hear them on their radio frequencies. We stayed there for one night and one day. After that our command told us we were not an occupying force but a protective force and told us to retreat to Camp Hadrian. But when we arrived back at the base we heard that the Chutu crossing was overrun by Taliban. That meant that the Taliban could infiltrate our area. The next day, we had the assignment to recon [conduct reconnaissance on] the road to Cemetery Hill. I was assigned with the infantry, travelling in a Mercedes-Benz soft-top truck. I was sitting in the back. We were the first vehicle. After us came two Patrias [Finnish-built armored personnel vehicles]. The rest of the platoon took another road to check out. While we were traveling we approached an S-turn." Schoonhoven points to the paper with the pen. "At the end of the S-turn we could see three scooters coming our way. They suddenly fell to the ground. We thought it was an accident but the drivers and passengers immediately ran into the gully and opened fire. It all happened in a split second and was very confusing. The person in front of me, Sergeant Beekman, got hit. He dropped into the driver's lap and the gunner started firing his machine gun but there was a problem with the gun. At that point I tried to start firing, but bullets were flying everywhere and I could hear them buzzing near my head, only missing me by an inch. Meanwhile, the trouble with the machine gun was that a Taliban bullet had hit the lid and it got jammed. The gunner fixed the problem and started firing again. We wanted to get out of there because the distance between us and the enemy was only twenty meters. The problem was that the two Patria vehicles were behind us in the S-turn"—Schoonhoven draws their position on my pad—"so they could not offer any support and couldn't turn properly because the road was too small. So we were stuck between the Taliban and our colleagues in the Patrias." He emphasizes the point by drawing their position on the pad, boxed in between the two. "Eventually the Patria drivers managed to slowly drive back through the S-turn in reverse, so we could retreat. While we were retreating I looked to the right and there were a couple of kids watching the fight, sitting on a wall, hands covering their ears while bullets were flying by and hitting the wall they were sitting on. Our driver tried to reverse, but we got stuck in a ditch. Sergeant Beekman, who was wounded, got out of the truck to guide us out of the ditch and I decided to jump out to stand between my colleagues and the enemy to support them. One of the Taliban was walking towards a wall with a small opening in it. He tried to aim at us through the opening and at that point I got a clear shot at his head and killed him. Just before I pulled the trigger there was a short moment when our eyes met. There were only ten meters between me and him so I could see the bullet entering his skull. Meanwhile the driver had managed to turn our truck in the right direction but not all the Patrias were reversed properly. While they were turning I walked behind the vehicles to protect them. Then I got into the car and we drove to a bridge, where we met the rest of the platoon and lighted up some cigarettes. Our medic looked at the sergeant's wounds and saw that fortunately his armored vest had saved him. We got into a defensive line and waited awhile for the enemy to retaliate, but they didn't show and we returned to base safely."

Back at the base, after the event, Schoonhoven tells me he was still feeling the adrenaline dump of close-quarters combat. He smoked three or four cigarettes in a row. He says to this day he still sees the Taliban's face and thinks of the mist of blood that exploded from behind the wall after he pulled the trigger. It looked like a balloon filled with flour, he thought, after the round hit, "poof," and then nothing more. Schoonhoven was awarded the Knight's Cross for his bravery, the third-highest award given by the Dutch military. The citation reads:

> Corporal Sebastiaan Schoonhoven received the decoration for his fearless conduct when he left his hit vehicle during an enemy attack near Shingowlah to give cover to his commanding officer (Sergeant Beekman) so that Beekman could direct the vehicle to a safe area. By putting his own life in danger he prevented casualties within his group.

"There was no time to digest it," Schoonhoven tells me, putting down the pad and mulling it over. "I would get manic sometimes after, but mostly when back at the base I'd listen to Nirvana and not think at all."

However, it wasn't Schoonhoven's first but rather his second kill, I learn, that haunted him long after his deployment in Afghanistan was over. He pauses again before telling the story. It started when his unit got word that the Taliban had taken over a school near the village of Shian Shan. Two Dutch platoons rolled out of Camp Hadrian to confront the Taliban fifteen kilometers to the north. This time Schoonhoven was manning a .50 caliber turret gun on a Patria armored personnel carrier. The convoy also had two other Patrias, eight Mercedes-Benz trucks and two Swedish-made troop carriers called YPRs. It was a lot of firepower, but these Dutch soldiers already knew that in a fight with the Taliban more is always better. As they approached the village, Schoonhoven and his fellow soldiers saw civilians moving in the opposite direction, a bad sign. They saw Pashto graffiti on a mud wall.* Their Afghan interpreter told them what it said: "Fuck NATO."

"We knew the shit was going to hit the fan any minute," Schoonhoven tells me.

One hundred meters outside the village, Schoonhoven's vehicle dropped two four-man fireteams out of the back, then pulled up to a plateau near the Helmand River to provide overwatch protection for them. Within moments they were taking Taliban mortar fire. The mortars signaled the start of the ambush, followed by heavy machine-gun fire from the

---

* Pashto and Dari are the two official languages of Afghanistan, with Pashto being used primarily by the Pashtun people prevalent in southern Afghanistan and Dari widely spoken in the northern, western and central regions of the country.

northeast. The Taliban were using Russian-made "Dushka" machine guns, so nicknamed because of the low "*dush, dush*" belly-exhaling sound they make when being fired.

Soon the Dutch were dodging rocket-propelled grenades coming from the village graveyard. The Taliban's three-pronged attack dissected the Dutch unit, pinning the soldiers down with fields of fire to the north and south. The Dutch units returned fire, but they were also badly exposed. Schoonhoven swung his .50 cal toward the graveyard and fired a burst. The first rounds plowed up the ground in front of the Taliban firing positions. Taliban continued popping up around the graveyard, firing down on Dutch troops. Schoonhoven aimed a bit higher, took a breath and pulled the trigger; he saw the silhouette of a fighter go down. Yeah! Got another one, he thought to himself initially, but then realized how small the shape was compared to the others. But there was no time to think; his commander was yelling to him that there were three men in the trees above the graveyard. He pivoted the big gun, put the tree in his sights and held down the trigger until the last of the belt ran through the feeder. When the dust cleared, he could see the entire tree was gone, and so was his ammo. The Taliban were still firing.

"I can hear the *ting, ting, ting* of AK rounds hitting us," says Schoonhoven, "but I need to get out of the turret and onto the outside of the vehicle to reload."

He waited for the Taliban guns to go silent for a moment, then counted to himself, three, two, one, just to be sure they were reloading. He sprang from the hatch, fresh ammo belts in hand; opened the top of the .50 cal; threaded the rounds through the receiver; closed the weapon; and scurried back into his hole, all within ten seconds. Schoonhoven's Patria positioned itself to cover the infantry it had dropped off and now hurried them back into the protection of the vehicle, which pulled to a safer position. The Dutch regrouped and began firing mortars of their own around a house where a large group of twenty to twenty-five Taliban had taken cover. An air strike was called. Forward air controllers painted the house with their lasers and within minutes a JDAM (joint direct attack munition) missile obliterated it.

"Everyone starts yelling, 'Fuck yeah,'" says Schoonhoven. After running into a well-planned ambush, the Dutch soldiers shook off the surprise, defaulted to their training and forced the Taliban out of the village. After holding their positions for a while, the Dutch soldiers moved into the village to look for bodies. While they didn't find any, they did find something else that was disturbing. Schoonhoven says that the Taliban had a prisoner they had captured earlier and, judging by the marks on his body, tortured. His hands and feet were chained together, Schoonhoven says. He was in bad shape but still alive.

Back at the base, Schoonhoven thought, I survived another one. He felt almost untouchable now, but even more detached from himself. He'd get no sleep at all that night.

"At that point I'm not really sure how I feel," Schoonhoven tells me, taking a cigarette from my pack on the table, lighting it and inhaling deeply. "I didn't really think about it until we were sitting around the base talking about the battle and another soldier confessed that he had fired at a Taliban that looked smaller than the others. It made me think about the one I had shot."

"What was it that bothered you about it?" I ask, pressing him.

"Was it a boy?" he blurts out suddenly. "Did I kill a boy, not a man?"

He looks away. But because there was no body to find he'll never really know the truth. The not-knowing, he says, is almost worse for him.

"All of us soldiers know what it's like to kill," he says, "but it's easier to talk to people that have been there." He draws a little circle in the air with his free hand, indicating this place, Bonaire, a crystal-blue bubble in the south Caribbean, which, with a few exceptions besides Schoonhoven and myself, lies untouched by the war in Afghanistan.

"Most people don't know what happened over there. I like that not everyone knows. I'm here for my rest. I'm trying to forget it."

"Do you think you'll be able to?"

"No," he answers immediately, "but perhaps I can squeeze it into a smaller space in here," he says, pointing to his head, "and put it away."

He admits that even here on this island that was supposed to give him refuge, he hasn't been so successful. Sometimes he drinks too much, despite stomach problems that indicate he shouldn't drink at all. He tells me about one night when a woman kept pushing him to give her his seat at the bar. She became annoying to the point where he lost all patience.

"At that moment I was in Afghanistan in my head. That's why I couldn't take it and I snapped."

He began flinging over plastic tables until the staff and other male patrons got him under control, finally ejecting him from the bar.

Part of what bothers him, he says, is the same complaint that I've heard from so many other troops returning from combat, that civilians might have curiosity, but deep down they don't really care or don't really want to know. His eyes begin to glisten as he remembers that night.

"I think it's not on me to say something. To me it's not worth all the energy to remember and tell the stories over and over. It gets irritating." He pauses, takes a drag of his cigarette; he releases its blue smoke as if it's a furtive memory, escaping without being told.

"But people should know something," he says suddenly, with conviction. "Dutch people also fight . . . they kill and they get killed . . . and they get wounded."

While in the army, a fellow soldier and scuba instructor taught Schoonhoven how to dive. He became so enamored with the sport that he moved up in certifications until he was made a dive master, able to help train and lead other scuba divers. He loved diving because it was a place where he didn't have to talk, where he could leave his wars behind.

"You're flying through a different world," he says, "one that not everyone sees. I feel very peaceful there. It's a peaceful place."

He stops and laughs, thinking of something else. "But not on night dives; that's when everything comes out to hunt. There's a lot of killing going on then." He smiles, thinking of the barracuda and other predators that gather around the rusting hull of the *Hilma Hooker,* Bonaire's largest and shallowest wreck dive and a favorite of night divers.

AT KARPATA, WE FOLLOW the chain deeper. At 120 feet, I stage my nitrox cylinder on a nest of rocks to pick up on my ascent. At 150 feet my dive computer is already beginning to beep, warning me that I've gone beyond the established, if somewhat arbitrary, 130-foot limit of recreational diving. Schoonhoven and I glance at each other and both of us make a pronounced "okay" with our thumbs and forefingers to signal we're good to continue, no problems. At 200 feet the sloping angle of the reef becomes vertical and this world of water becomes almost silent except for the iron-lung-like sounds of my inhalation and exhalation through my regulator. For a sense of security, I hold the mouthpiece of a second regulator, my backup, attached to a second air cylinder clipped to my chest on the D-rings of my buoyancy compensator device, or BCD. The BCD is a harness with a U-shaped bladder that I can fill with air or deflate to achieve neutral buoyancy, a kind of equilibrium where I neither rise nor fall but suspend myself in the water. I'm not so worried about my regulator failing, but I know that a rupture in the tiny plastic part called an O-ring, which costs only pennies but helps maintain the life-giving seal between the regulator and

the airflow from the cylinder, could be fatal. I wonder, however, as my limbs become heavier with every foot we descend,
whether I will even be able to find my mouth with the backup
if I need to. I'm already starting to feel some of the strange
gauziness of nitrogen narcosis, a drunk-like state many divers
begin to experience at depth. I look over at Schoonhoven; I can
see in his eyes, he's calm, relaxed, but I can tell he's not sure
he sees the same thing in mine. Still, we give each other the
"okay" sign another time as we continue down the wall.

Now my world has become the narrow tunnel that I can
see from my mask. My breathing and my beeping computer
(warning me I've gone beyond, way beyond, my recreational
diving depth) seem to me like a vitals cart next to a hospital
bed, signaling the patient is still alive. We descend through several thermoclines, layers of increasingly colder water, before we
reach the bottom of the wall. We stand for a moment, looking
out at the darkness that separates us like a black curtain, but
we go deeper still. I look at my computer. It reads 296 feet.
I look at Schoonhoven as he peers into the darkness. Is this
the place where one need never think of war again? Or is it
farther still? I move forward, seeking only four more feet, a
benchmark number, but an arm waves me back. It does, at
that moment, seem like the small membrane of difference
between living and being lost in the blackness below. But the
blackness, while devastatingly lonely, still beckons. I wonder if
the pressure would envelop me like a snug blanket if I tipped
past the edge into its seductive void. Is this the place where
the world above and the past can't find us? My considerations

seem infinite but last, in reality, only a few moments. I look at Schoonhoven. There is no time for uncertainty or lingering. This is a "bounce" dive, the risky practice of touching a depth beyond the normal recreational limits but not spending enough time there to require extensive decompression. You "bounce" off the bottom and go up. Spending even a few minutes on the bottom can mean running out of breathing gas in the shallows as we decompress. Doing so could mean we both get bent, wracked by nitrogen bubbles expanding inside our tissues and organs. We also risk pulmonary and cerebral embolism, larger bubbles that can block our blood vessels to our lungs and brain, killing us. We need to go. Schoonhoven jerks his thumb upward—the sign to ascend. Slowly, we begin swimming toward the surface, controlling our ascent, making sure not to outrace our air bubbles. While it was easy floating down, the wall seems steeper now. I press the auto-inflator button on my BCD to add a little air into the bladder, giving me a tiny lift, but am careful to not fill it too much, knowing the air will expand as the pressure decreases during our swim up. If it expands too much the BCD can take me on a rocket ride called a runaway ascent, which, again, has a good probability of ending ugly, especially considering the depth from which we just bounced. I pick up my nitrox cylinder and at ninety feet, we stop at the mouth of a cave and make the gas switch from regular air to the higher-oxygen-content nitrox, the logic being more oxygen in our bodies' cells pushes out harmful residual nitrogen, helping us to "off-gas" faster. At thirty feet we begin a full half hour of decompression, swimming in circles and exploring the now-shallow bottom of the shoreline, to help us while away the time before we can surface and talk excitedly about what we've just done and survived. It was a brief return to the type of adrenaline rush that Schoonhoven and I both experienced during combat, but this time there were no bombs or bullets. Yet, it was just as dangerous, perhaps more so at times, than some of what we experienced in war. When we reach the top, we're elated, psyched about our accomplishment, high-fiving each other. The celebration will be short. Later, a young colleague who came with us to act as a safety diver tells the assistant manager of the dive shop we both work for what we did with our day off. While we have a right to kill ourselves with our cowboy shenanigans if we need to, we're told, we don't have a right to do it using the shop's gear and risking the shop's reputation.

While we lived through the dive, our jobs are now in jeopardy. Only through profuse apologies do we both avoid getting fired, and we will both be in the penalty box for several weeks. The gravity of our recklessness is compounded the next day, when another diver dies at Karpata, a victim not of deep diving but a reported pulmonary embolism. This diver found death but, unlike us, wasn't looking for it. Because I pushed to make the dive, I begin to feel guilty about the fallout for Schoonhoven. It's true he's a big boy and able to make his own decisions, but he probably doesn't need the added temptation of reckless endeavors dangled in front of him daily by someone who is supposed to be listening to his stories, not egging him on to new ones. However, he does not hold it against me.

Despite our foolishness, we now have a bond that goes beyond our shared war zone experiences. Together we experienced the danger but also the solitude and peace of the deep. There is, we know, a bond of loyalty to each other in that as well.

A few days before I leave Bonaire to return to the United States and begin my fellowship at Harvard, I ask Schoonhoven why he agreed to share his stories with me for my book. He looks down, gathers his thoughts and sighs.

"I want a job where I can make okay money, enough to support my family and my [future] kids," he says to me. "If there is a book with my memories in it, then I don't have to hold them in my head; at least that's what I hope."

POSTSCRIPT

After the birth of their first child, a daughter named Robyn, Sebastiaan and Carolien Schoonhoven returned to the Netherlands. A year and a half later they had their second child, a son named Finn.

The photograph of the author's wife he carried in his helmet
during his last reporting trip to Afghanistan

EPILOGUE

DEUS EX MACHINA

> And sometimes remembering will lead to a story, which
> makes it forever. That's what stories are for. Stories are
> for joining the past to the future. Stories are for those
> late hours in the night when you can't remember how
> you got from where you were to where you are. Stories
> are for eternity, when memory is erased, when there is
> nothing to remember except the story.
>
> —Tim O'Brien, *The Things They Carried*

IN MY initial reporting and writing of this book, I was troubled that the stories featured here might collectively represent an indictment against hope. I'm glad to know now that
I was wrong. War both gives and takes from those most intimately involved in it. It wrests from them delusions of innocence and reveals, as we've explored, a shadow self capable not
only of taking life but sometimes of finding fulfillment in the
process. This undoubtedly creates confusion for both soldiers
and the societies they fight for, as the seduction of violence

challenges self-perceptions and even our beliefs about our own humanity. Additionally, living in the midst of death, witnessing the killing of comrades and friends, suffering physical and psychological injuries, compounds this disequilibrium for warriors in the aftermath of battle. So how, then, does one go forward in a world marked by pain and loss, and steeped in the moral inconsistency that those capable of the greatest violence win?

The truth I've been able to discern from my interviews and personal experiences in war is the not-unfamiliar concept that it magnifies the duality of our nature—our capacity for good and propensity for evil—and has an unequaled power to unite and divide us, to fill us simultaneously with pride and shame. But the piece that we are only beginning to more fully embrace (out of necessity, with thousands of American troops returned or returning home from the wars in Iraq and Afghanistan) is that that same sense of duality can destroy us if we do not honestly share its full and complete narrative. As difficult and perhaps unnatural as it may be, that sharing must include giving voice to the natural excitement and fellowship of war as well as communalizing its grief.

Of the stories told here, there is hope in all, some in the ability to bear well the terrible responsibilities of killing in war, as in the case of Staff Sergeant Mikeal Auton; some in the promising results of the ongoing recovery process, as with Lance Corporal James Sperry; and others simply in the courage and willingness to explain what can happen to you once you pull the trigger, as in the case of the late Corporal William Wold. We owe all these men a debt, not simply for their service, but for their willingness to help us understand just a little bit better. We must implore and help the others who follow to do the same.

Fortunately, there is a thread of hope in my own story that was the result of this very thing—being willing to do the work of sharing my own fractured narrative and reconstructing a new one grounded in hope and purpose, instead of ending in self-destruction. Though I didn't know it at the time, it began almost comically, and with no other likely solution in sight, as my own personal deus ex machina, a god from a machine, the savior from the final act of a Greek tragedy, literally suspended from a series of ropes and pulleys.

Her name was Anita. We met in Joshua Tree National Park at a rock-climbing class in the summer of 2008. At only four foot eleven she had what most would consider an understandable fear of heights, yet as was her style, it was something she was ready to take on without hesitation, like the many other challenges she had already dispatched in her life. We had a natural banter, chatting and laughing. At one point during the class, she put her hands on her hips in a feigned sign of impatience, asking me why it was taking me twice as long as the others to tie the knot that I would use to "belay" her, or anchor her against a possible fall as she climbed. I looked at her as if she was crazy and told her that this was quite obviously the one knot she might want me to take the time to get right.

It felt very much like flirting and probably was, at least on my part, but we were both in other relationships. We became friends instead, meeting for dinner or drinks with our significant others in tow but focusing our conversations on each other.

We talked at a frantic pace like two idiots bailing out a row-boat. Later, I invited her to hike Temescal Canyon with me and another friend. My girlfriend at the time chose not to go. Over the course of three hours, amid breathtaking vistas of the Pacific, Anita and I again spoke nonstop. There was more to this feisty Filipina, I learned, than just her sarcasm and expensive boots.

After an American sailor married her mother, she came to the U.S. at age thirteen and learned to speak English by watching *General Hospital* on TV. Despite his strict discipline, she became close to her adopted father, learning to love sports as he did, especially his hometown football and baseball teams, the Patriots and the Red Sox. She became a successful advertising executive, married her college sweetheart and had a daughter, but divorced just two years after her birth. I admired her strength and tenacity and was enthralled by the oversized personality that fit inside the travel-sized woman. When my relationship with my girlfriend ended shortly before I left Los Angeles for my fellowship at Harvard, I tried to reconnect with Anita but ran out of time. And so began what should've been a year of enlightenment, meeting accomplished fellow journalists and immersing myself in the myriad of offerings at America's preeminent institution of higher learning, but instead I traveled down what I consider the long, dark corridor of my life.

IF THERE WAS ANYTHING that underscored the fact that I needed therapy to deal with the toxic blowback that became my life in the aftermath of my war experiences, it was this: during a holiday break from my fellowship, while doing coke with an old friend, we turned the razor we used to chop the lines onto our own bodies. I pulled it along my lower back, the blood immediately bleeding up from the fissure I had just created below and parallel to my waistline, where it would be hidden from all but those who knew me most intimately. My friend did the same. Then I took the razor again and this time sank it in above my right hip deeply enough to carve a long asterisk that, in time, raised into a permanent dark-pink keloid. I'm not sure what statement I was making, but it may have had something to do with the desperation of feeling like an asterisk to history.

Cutting didn't become a regular practice for me. It was more of a novelty than a persistent desire, simply another chance to physically punish myself for letting a man die.

What was almost comically incomprehensible to me after the realization of what I had done in Fallujah was that my dreams before I began going to war with great frequency were mostly filled with the idea of saving people rather than letting them die. I remember a specific dream I had when I lived in Washington, DC, in which I dived into the frozen Potomac after a jet crashed in the river (likely spurred by the memory of an Air Florida plane crashing into the river in 1982 and the bystander who jumped into the icy water in an attempt to rescue someone; seventy-eight people died). In my dream I took a cable from a construction crane on the riverbank and wrapped it around my waist, swam to the plane, looped it around the fuselage and then used the crane to

winch the plane and its passengers to safety back on shore . . .
No big thing.

But when the actual opportunity to save someone was
right in front of me, a man begging for his life, I couldn't see it.
I was shocked and confused by the killing I had just witnessed
and videotaped. I couldn't process the fact that the person in
front of me might be the next victim. If there was any doubt
that the shooting I captured on video was unjustified, it disappeared completely with Taleb Salem Nidal. Wounded and
obviously unarmed, he was killed in a horrible and cowardly
way, almost two dozen bullets stitching his back, likely as he
saw the intent of his killers and tried in vain to crawl away.
While I can never forgive myself for this, what I did realize
was that I had been aggressively trying to kill myself, either in
combat or through the attrition of alcohol, drugs and dangerous situations, in atonement.

If it accomplished anything, the cutting proved to me how
far off the grid I had fallen. In its aftermath, I finally succumbed to therapy, but only because of a confluence of circumstances. A friend, despite being treated shoddily by me, helped
find me a suitable therapist, and the therapist was willing to
treat me for a fraction of his normal fee. But perhaps most
importantly, I felt I had a reason to go. While still at Harvard
I had made a trip back to Los Angeles for some interviews for
this book. While there, I contacted Anita. We hiked Temescal
Canyon again and then I made her dinner. On the plane back
to Boston, I wrote her a five-page e-mail, explaining how from
the very first day that I met her at Joshua Tree she had inspired

me with her courage and willingness to face her greatest fears. Then I really piled it on like a lovesick schoolboy, using our climbing experience as the metaphor for how I would always be there to protect her from a fall. It took her three days to respond. I began to think I might've overshot a little. I wondered if I had not only lost the potential of a romantic relationship but killed the friendship as well. After some lengthy "negotiations" and a number of cross-country visits we began a relationship that resulted in our getting an apartment together in Los Angeles. But it would not be just the two of us. Anita's ten-year-old daughter would also be living with us, as well as Anita's sister (who was going through a messy divorce) and her six-year-old daughter. Overnight, I became a parent. The car wreck of post-traumatic stress and drug and alcohol abuse was no longer an option, nor would it be tolerated by Anita.

For two months, I embarked on a life I had never experienced before; each morning I woke up and made breakfast for the girls and then drove them to school. I helped them with their homework, played board games and card games with them, watched the Disney Channel and listened to them speak about the virtues of the Jonas Brothers and Justin Bieber. At night I would make them dinner and when Anita got home from work, we sat down at the table together as a family, one to which I was joined not by blood but by belief.

Of all that I had accomplished, my time in this family, I quickly realized, was an irreplaceable gift, the opportunity and motivation to be a better man. But the anger, guilt and self-destruction did not simply disappear with my new life and responsibilities. I had a difficult path ahead and many months before I could begin to let go of the past and fully embrace hope.

Shortly after the invasion of Iraq in the spring of 2003 and one year before the mosque shootings, I was briefly captured by Saddam's Fedayeen militia along with a CNN colleague, our bodyguard and an interpreter outside Tikrit. It's strange to me, because while I was scared shitless at the time, in the subsequent years I rarely thought about the capture and didn't think it had contributed to my erratic postwar state of mind. But there was a place, I discovered through my eventual therapy, where it did intersect, a place I avoided, until I could no longer contain the toxic mess of my life.

This is the image that I've tried to forget: I'm on my knees and I'm pleading for my life. As I was taught in a hostile-environment course for journalists, which I was compelled to take by my employer long after I started covering wars for a living, I'm trying to make eye contact with one of my captors. I'm trying to make him see me as a fellow human being rather than an animal, a threat, an impediment or even leverage. My hands are clasped one on top of the other and I pump them in front of me as if I might be agitating a bottle of champagne after winning the Tour de France or Indy 500—but this, I hope instead, he will recognize as the international symbol of someone begging for his life. In case he still doesn't understand, in perhaps an ill-advised gesture, I draw one hand across my throat like a blade and at the same time say in English, "No. No."

Sitting in my therapist's office six years later, I wondered why I had shut out so completely this specific detail of the memory. Was I ashamed of what I had done? Was I afraid to remember what it felt like to be completely powerless and without any control? Or was it, as my therapist asked me to consider, a correlation of two images too disturbing for me to hold together in my mind: the image of myself pleading with my captors for my life compared with the image of Taleb Salem Nidal inside that Fallujah mosque pleading with me to save his? While I got out of my predicament alive, thanks to the negotiations of Tofiq Abdol, my Kurdish interpreter, Nidal was not fortunate enough to have someone like that to champion his cause.

CONSIDERING HIS CAREER CHOICE, Mark Sadoff was aptly and whimsically named. He had treated everyone from husbands and wives trying to comprehend their loveless relationships to Central American victims of torture. He had been studying an emerging form of therapy known as EMDR, eye movement desensitization and reprocessing therapy (the same therapy used in Michael Ayala's case). With EMDR the therapist attempts to re-create the rapid eye movement of sleep by having the patient follow the therapist's finger moving back and forth in front of his eyes like a metronome. At the same time the therapist prompts the patient to talk about the incident affecting them, trying to change its negative orbit into something more positive. In my situation, Dr. Sadoff asked me if I purposely wanted Taleb Salem Nidal to die or if my actions were accidental, rather than intentional. If I could have prevented his death, if I knew what would've happened to him when I left the room, would I have acted differently? Of course I would have stayed, I said, I would have taken him out of the mosque to somewhere he might be safe, rather than leaving him alone. It was Dr. Sadoff's effort to get my guilt-addled brain to understand that Taleb Salem Nidal hadn't registered as a victim to me, as someone who needed saving. The person I was trying to save, by exposing the crime, was the one who had already been killed on videotape in front of me. He helped me to understand that it was a mistake, not malice. My intentions were good, I just hadn't thought the situation through clearly, which was understandable considering what I had just witnessed. Through our discussions he also helped me to see that difficult but ultimately critical connection between my capture outside Tikrit and the murder of Taleb Salem Nidal. With no interpreter, no Tofiq, as I had had during my capture, to translate for him, Nidal would die because I did not understand, as I should have, that I needed to walk him out of that mosque under my protection. I didn't save anyone, as I did in my dream; I let the plane sink to the bottom of the Potomac. I did nothing. But I had to find a way to forgive myself, or in a misguided search for equal justice, I would end up killing myself in exchange.

Shortly after Anita and I moved in together I began preparing for a reporting trip to Afghanistan. It would be my fourth time there, and I stepped up my therapy sessions, hoping to find some closure before I went. I found myself telling

Dr. Sadoff that one of the ways in which I thought I might be able to be at peace with my actions in Fallujah was if I lost a limb during the upcoming trip, preferably a leg, rather than a hand or arm. The loss of that leg, while not a life, could make me feel that I was even for Nidal; that, along with my years of self-hatred and self-destruction, would ante up for his life.

But while Dr. Sadoff couldn't dissuade me of the notion, my actual behavior during that reporting trip to Afghanistan was the anathema of all that I had been saying. For the summer I was in Afghanistan, I trod perhaps more carefully than I ever had in my life, walking well-worn paths and being careful to stay out of clearings and the line of fire when possible. I had purchased a Kevlar helmet and body armor, which I normally never wore while working in war zones. Inside the helmet, I placed a picture of Anita, and inside the body armor, a photograph of each of the girls, one in front and one in back. Somehow, I understood there was now a value to my life that went beyond myself. If I died or lost a limb, Nidal and I might be even, but I would then be cheating the people who now considered me part of their family, the ones I wore next to my heart and on top of my head. My past actions during war didn't make me a bad person, nor did they invalidate the good things inside me; they simply proved the existence of both. While I obviously had not always seen clearly what was the right thing to do in the past, in this case, I had no doubt. Despite all my shortcomings, all my betrayals, all the pain I caused, all my sins, I wanted to come home alive—yes, changed by the things war had both given and taken from me, but somehow complete.

POSTSCRIPT

I secretly married Anita exactly two years to the day I met her at Joshua Tree, three days before leaving for my fourth trip to Afghanistan. I married her again, in front of family and friends, after my return. Inscribed on my wedding band is the Latin phrase *"Ex tenebris lux"*—"Out of darkness, light."

ONGOING STORYTELLING EFFORT

If you have comments about this book and are a service member or veteran (from anywhere in the world) who would like to be part of an ongoing veterans' storytelling effort, please e-mail me at the address below. Your story, photos, or video may be shared in this book's companion website.

thingstheycannotsay@gmail.com

The author's mother and father (right) during the Korean War

ACKNOWLEDGMENTS

MY DEEPEST thanks to all the service personnel, both U.S. and international, who had the courage and generous hearts to share their most intimate stories of war. Your efforts, I strongly believe, will help you on your journey—and encourage others to find their own way home again. They include those featured in this book: Michael Ayala, Mikeal Auton, Joe Caley, Morris Goins, Zach Iscol, Thomas Saal, Sebastiaan Schoonhoven, Leonard Shelton, James Sperry, Lior Tailer and William Wold.

My thanks also to the many others who helped me to understand the combatant's experience in war, especially past and current service members: Frederick Coe, Wil Cromie, Pat Donahue, Justin Featherstone, Bernard Finestone, Dana Golan, Phillip Herbig, Roxanne Hurley, Gord Jenkins, Jeff Milhorn, Cathy Murphy, Arthur Myers, Zakyia Ibrahim Rahman, Matthew Rodgers, John Schluep, Justin Schmidt, Jonathan Staab, Sean Tuckey, Garret Ware and Joe Young.

I talked with the mothers, wives and girlfriends of some

of the combatants profiled here—and I thank them for their contributions—but out of respect for their privacy, I will not name them here.

Several experts in the field of combat-related post-traumatic stress disorder provided invaluable assistance both through their written works and in personal interviews they granted to me, and in some cases, they helped me to make contact with individuals featured in this book. I'm extremely grateful to Dr. Edward Tick, author of *War and the Soul: Healing Our Nation's Veterans from Post-Traumatic Stress Disorder,* and to his assistant Paula Griffin. I'm also indebted to Dr. Jonathan Shay, author of *Achilles in Vietnam: Combat Trauma and the Undoing of Character* and *Odysseus in America: Combat Trauma and the Trials of Homecoming.* Lieutenant Colonel Dave Grossman was very helpful in providing insight into the actual combat experience both in direct interviews with me and in his seminal work *On Killing: The Psychological Cost of Learning to Kill in War and Society* and his follow-up work, *On Combat: The Psychology and Physiology of Deadly Conflict in War and in Peace.* Particularly helpful in quantifying the impact of combat on our society was the RAND Corporation's study "Invisible Wounds of War: Psychological and Cognitive Injuries, Their Consequences, and Services to Assist Recovery," edited by Terri Tanielian and Lisa Jaycox. And all those of us who have become students of war know the debt we owe to J. Glenn Gray and his work *The Warriors: Reflections on Men in Battle* for taking the subject out of the realm of myth and bringing it back to earth for honest discussion.

Other books that provided critical perspectives and thoughtful insights: *War Is a Force That Gives Us Meaning* and *What Every Person Should Know About War*, both by the brilliant Chris Hedges; *War* by the excessively talented Sebastian Junger; Anthony Loyd's dually devastating and inspiring tome *My War Gone By, I Miss It So*; Ryszard Kapuscinski's classic *The Soccer War*; *One Soldier's War* by Arkady Babchenko, which provides a grunt's eye view from a Russian perspective; Brian Turner's *Phantom Noise*, which exemplifies the warrior-poet ideal; and the enduring standards of military strategy and tactics *On War* by Karl von Clausewitz, *The Art of War* by Niccolò Machiavelli and the work of the same name by Sun Tzu; *Breaking the Silence: Soldiers' Testimonies from Hebron and Women's Soldiers' Testimonies*; and finally, perhaps the most important American novel to explore the Vietnam War experience and one whose stories and title helped inspire this book, Tim O'Brien's *The Things They Carried*. And I'd like to offer special thanks to author and Vietnam War veteran Karl Marlantes for his remarkable book *What It Is Like to Go to War*, which is one of the most enlightening works on the subject I've ever read and which was instrumental in helping me to both identify and better endure the burdens of my own wars.

Many thanks to Hannah Catabia for her research work in the U.S., to Stephanie Freid for her research and interview assistance in Israel and to Mohammed Jalizadi for his efforts on my behalf in northern Iraq.

I want to express my gratitude to the Nieman Foundation

for the fellowship opportunity that afforded me a paid year to struggle and reflect and eventually complete this difficult, emotional and cathartic project. Specifically I'm grateful to my colleague and friend Audra Ang, who tracked down the therapist who succeeded in derailing my plans for martyrdom on the twin altars of self-absorption and self-indulgence.

I'm extremely fortunate to have a very supportive imprint in Harper Perennial; my friend and editor Amy Baker is as encouraging of my efforts as she is forgiving of my lapsed deadlines. She made this a better book. And also with the Harper Perennial team, much appreciation to editor Michael Signorelli for taking the project handoff seamlessly and getting it across the finish line, and to production editor Mary Beth Constant and copyeditor Aja Pollock, who transformed this sometimes unwieldy manuscript from a jumble of words into a readable format where verb tenses actually exist in their proper time and place.

Finally, my thanks to my wife, Anita—whose unqualified support and example of courage and perseverance in the face of adversity inspire me and who is now helping me exercise muscle memory in the habit of trying to do the right thing daily.

I'd like to leave readers with this last passage, which I first read in Chris Hedges's book *War Is a Force That Gives Us Meaning* after coming home from the War in Iraq. It's a simple but important message, one I hope never to forget:

"We are tempted to reduce life to a simple search for happiness. Happiness, however, withers if there is no meaning. But to live only for meaning—indifferent to all happiness—makes us fanatic, self-righteous, and cold. It leaves us cut off from our own humanity and the humanity of others. We must hope for grace, for our lives to be sustained by moments of meaning and happiness, both equally worthy of human communion."

BOOKS BY KEVIN SITES

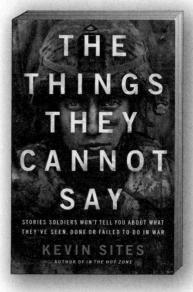

THE THINGS THEY CANNOT SAY

Stories Soldiers Won't Tell You About What They've Seen, Done or Failed to Do in War

ISBN 978-0-06-199052-6 (paperback)

Eleven soldiers and Marines display a rare courage that transcends battlefield heroics—they share the truth about their wars. For each of them it means something different: one struggles to recover from a head injury he believes has stolen his ability to love, another attempts to make amends for the killing of an innocent man, while yet another finds respect for the enemy fighter who tried to kill him. Award-winning journalist and author Kevin Sites asks the difficult questions of these combatants, many of whom he first met while in Afghanistan and Iraq and others he sought out from different wars: What is it like to kill? What is it like to be under fire? How do you know what's right? What can you never forget?

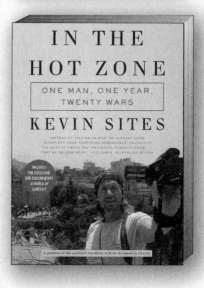

IN THE HOT ZONE

One Man, One Year, Twenty Wars

ISBN 978-0-06-122875-9 (paperback)

Kevin Sites is a man on a mission. Armed with just a video camera, a digital camera, a laptop, and a satellite modem, the award-winning journalist begins his journey with the anarchic chaos of Somalia in September 2005 and ends with the Israeli-Hezbollah war in the summer of 2006. Sites talks with rebels and government troops, child soldiers and child brides, and features the people on every side, including those caught in the cross fire. His honest reporting helps destroy the myths of war by putting a human face on war's inhumanity. Personally, Sites will come to discover that the greatest danger he faces may not be from bombs and bullets, but from the unsettling power of the truth.

"These images and dispatches from the numberless rooms of hell have an undeniable cumulative power."
—*Kirkus Reviews*

Visit www.AuthorTracker.com for exclusive information on your favorite HarperCollins authors.

Available wherever books are sold, or call 1-800-331-3761 to order.